Heartsong

Heartsong

Living with a Dying Heart

A Memoir

Anita Swanson Speake

SHE WRITES PRESS

Published 2019
Printed in the United States of America
ISBN: 978-1-63152-437-0 pbk
ISBN: 978-1-63152-438-7 ebk
Library of Congress Control Number: 2018961524

For information, address:
She Writes Press
1569 Solano Ave #546
Berkeley, CA 94707

She Writes Press is a division of SparkPoint Studio, LLC.

If suffering alone taught, then all the world would be wise. To suffering must be added mourning, understanding, and patience . . .

—Anne Morrow Lindbergh

Preface

Wwe were hiking. Walking, really. It was something my husband and I did often, but this morning was especially promising. The recent warm weather and snow melt had given us reason to hope that the mountains just might be showing off. Creek beds, dry and rocky in the summer, would now be filled with crystal clear water rushing down the canyon. Snowcapped summits near our home, if winter had worked its magic, would be sending a waterfall tumbling over the cliff.

And so we walked with anticipation—but I, as usual, was worried.

"Here's the deal," I said, slightly out of breath. "What if I wake up dead tomorrow morning?"

It wasn't an everyday question to ask my husband, but then again, I didn't have an everyday diagnosis.

With great patience, G tried to reassure me. "You're not going to wake up dead tomorrow morning or any other morning for that matter."

"But I *could*," I insisted. "And then you'd be upset and sad about the fact that I'd died, and you'd have to call the girls, who'd be all upset and sad as well, and everything would just be a mess. Sometimes I wake up in the middle of the night and stay awake for as long as I can just to prove to myself that I haven't died yet."

My husband looked skeptical.

"It's true!" I cried. "And then when the morning comes, and I realize I've made it through to another day, I give God a big shout-out." I glanced over at him. "Now, you would probably think it would end there, but it doesn't. This whole worrying thing starts up all over again with a brand-new day. It's hard, G. It's really hard."

"Well, if it makes you feel any better," he said evenly, "I think you should know that I don't worry about it all."

I stopped walking and stared him in disbelief. "You don't?"

He stopped too. "No, I don't. Would you like me to tell you why?"

"Yes. Yes. I would."

"Because the doctors have said your heart is responding to the medication. It's getting stronger, and I think you're going to just continue to get better."

"Hmm . . ." I said, not convinced.

This am-I-living-or-am-I-dying had turned out to be tricky business. G believed the doctors, but these facts remained: without the meds that sometimes worked and sometimes didn't, my heart would die. And I, of course, would go along with it.

However, on this particular morning, G's optimism was infectious, and so for the moment I gave in. We were walking. It was springtime in the mountains, and I was still alive.

"Let's keep going." G placed his hand beneath my elbow and urged me onward. "We can walk and talk about your worries at the same time."

I started moving, albeit a bit reluctantly.

"Let me ask you something," G said. "Did anyone ever tell you that you could wake up dead?"

I shook my head. "No."

"So your mind just made this up?"

"Yes. Well, not exactly. When I worked in the emergency room, the paramedics would often tell stories. Some of them were about the early-morning runs they'd make for people who'd gone to bed and never woken up. They'd say things like, 'Yeah, we had a lot of woke-up-dead calls this morning.'"

"Okay. Fine. So the paramedics told you stories. I just think that your medication is buying you time. Lots of time. Maybe even decades." Again, G urged me onward. "We're almost there. I think I hear the creek." He sounded excited. "The water level must be really high."

I encouraged my husband with a smile, but my thoughts took off in another direction. There were days when my coping mechanisms worked exceedingly well, but this was not one of them. My fear of dying kept darting in and out. One minute I was fine and the next minute I wasn't.

My cardiac diagnosis had stunned me. I wasn't ready for it; in fact, as it turned out, I wasn't ready for much of anything associated with disease or dying. But then who is, really?

I wasn't ready to leave G. I wasn't ready to leave my grown children or my young grandchildren. The thought of not being here for them was heartbreaking—and believe me, I know a thing or two about broken hearts.

Decades. G thought I had decades left to live.

I was hoping to just make it another year.

CHAPTER 1

You Want to Try That One More Time?

The cardiologist closed my chart. "You no longer have the luxury of time. I need you to get an angiogram sooner rather than later. It's impossible for me to tell what's really going on with your heart without it."

This particular cardiologist was a very tiny woman who wore a pristine white lab coat that threatened to consume her. Certainly, the sleeves were too long. They nearly covered up her fingertips, and the length of the coat far exceeded anything that said I should take her seriously. Her name, however, was embroidered in red script on her left shoulder, and that, along with all the initials that came after it, left little doubt: I needed to listen to what she was saying. Petite or not.

Now, what she'd said scared me. But did I believe her? No.

It has been a lifelong pattern of mine to minimize alarming news when I first hear it. Elizabeth Kübler-Ross called this Stage 1: Denial. I call it, You-Want-to-Run-That-By-Me-One-More-Time?

"Are you sure you read the right chart?" I asked after her big announcement.

"Are you Anita?"

"Yes."

"Then I have the right chart."

With that one simple statement, my mind slipped into gridlock, and within a matter of seconds I'd lost all ability to think. I could see Petite Cardiologist's lips moving, but I couldn't hear any sound coming out.

This new loss of ability to cope was extreme, even for me—mostly because for more than thirty years of my life I'd worked in adrenaline-filled areas of recovery rooms, intensive care units, and emergency rooms. In the decade before retiring from nursing, I'd been in charge of a small but busy emergency department on nights. Thinking fast on my feet was a skill that had come easily to me, and it was one at which I had excelled. I'd triaged and treated even the sickest patients with ease.

However, the passing years had changed everything. Now I was the patient who sat on the exam table, wearing the greatest human equalizer of all: the little blue-flowered patient gown. I had to fight just to keep my brain engaged in present time.

Almost against my will, my mind raced through a mental Rolodex. I was searching for an event that had happened years earlier.

Finally, I found it.

When I was a young nurse, I cared for a neurological patient who, after being told his brain tumor was inoperable, reached out and shook the resident's hand.

"Thank you so much for this good news," he said with a smile.

It took several minutes of back-and-forth conversation between the three of us before he fully understood the awful truth. His headaches were never going to go away.

So there I sat, much like my neurological patient from long ago, trying to misconstrue what the cardiologist had told me.

She pressed on. "Anita, I'm sorry. We need to get you scheduled for an angiogram immediately."

I wanted her to stop talking. Every time she opened up her mouth, bad news fell out. I pushed to rally my brain cells.

"Wait just a minute," I said. "You know, I only came here today because I happened to mention to my gynecologist on a simple little routine visit that growing old was turning into a real pain. It was her idea that I should get my shortness of breath checked out. I mean, lots of people have problems walking up hills, not just me." I felt my throat tighten. Still, I pushed on. "Are you saying that my heart is so bad I need to have an angiogram done right now? Everybody knows angiograms are a big deal. If you're going to inject dye through a wire into my heart, I need more time to get ready."

"Anita, you don't have the time," Petite Cardiologist said firmly. "Earlier, you mentioned that both of your parents died from heart disease."

"Yes, but—"

"I want to remind you that both the stress test and echogram showed you have something seriously wrong with your heart. We need to find out what that is. If we wait, it will only increase your chances for a heart attack." She shook her head. "You failed to complete the stress test. Remember? The one where we had you get on the treadmill and walk as far and as fast as you could? In addition to the stress test, the echogram showed us that your heart has become severely weakened."

"I know what a stress test and echogram are," I shot back.

"Well, you looked confused."

At last my frozen brain cells began to thaw. Still, I wasn't quite ready to play ball.

I thought about my husband—a physics major by education and a retired Aerospace senior vice president by achievement—who had left that morning on a consulting trip to Washington DC after I'd encouraged him to go.

"This is all so unnecessary," I'd said when he, yet again, asked me if he should cancel the trip. "You love going to DC." I gave him one of my best smiles. "Besides, the trip may be your only chance this year for you to play Mr. Big Shot." Confident that my medical issues were nonexistent, I continued reassuring him. "I'm still capable of getting a few cardiac tests done on my own."

He gave up asking. "Call me as soon as you know anything." He kissed me good-bye and walked out the door.

I wouldn't be able to reach him for hours.

Petite Cardiologist's voice pulled me back to reality. "I wouldn't say I consider you to be an emergency, but you are definitely urgent."

"Okay, but how urgent is urgent?"

She handed me a piece of paper. "I'd like to get it done before the end of the week. Call this number. They'll handle everything."

CHAPTER 2

This is Good News?

Four days later, G and I walked into the stark, modern, cavern-ous lobby of the UCLA Medical Center.

A large sign identified the room as the "Patient Waiting Area." No one else was there. Given the early-morning arrival time, the room's emptiness didn't surprise us. Still, the silence that filled the brightly lit space only heightened the seriousness of why I was there. There was no music being piped in. Neither were there any magazines lying about to distract waiting patients. Just the silence, and the occasional announcement over the PA system that indicated there was a code in progress somewhere in the hospital. I had to remind myself just to breathe.

It wasn't long before the nurse appeared at the entrance. When she called my name, I suddenly found myself filled with envy. I wanted to be the nurse calling out patient names, not the apprehensive-try-ing-to-act-as-if-everything-is-fine-patient who obediently followed her down the hall.

I was admitted into the pre-op area of the angio suite, and the nursing staff immediately moved into action. Monitors were hooked up, an intravenous bag was filled with fluid, and drugs began to drip their way into my system.

Everything moved along with such effortless efficiency that within minutes there was only one thing left for me to do: climb onto the gleaming stainless-steel gurney and let them wheel me down the hall.

The sedation drugs acted fast and were effective. Soon, the bright overhead lights and beeping monitor sounds of the angio suite were the only sights and sounds that cut through with razor-like clarity. Everything else was muddled, hazy, and far away.

Two hours later, Petite Cardiologist arrived at my beside in the recovery room with a smile on her face and my chart in her hand

"Anita." Her stern voice startled me awake. "I want to talk to you about your test results. I have good news to tell you. You have something called cardiomyopathy."

I stared up at her, my brain still in a fog.

"It's a general term for heart disease, but in your case it's specific to the left ventricle. It's the largest pumping mechanism of the human heart, and yours is sending out SOS signals. Of all the things you could have wrong, this is the best possible outcome. We have medication that we can give you. It will improve your heart function. Quite literally, these meds will act as a crutch for your heart."

I tried to listen to her, but the sedation drugs were still busy at work. It was impossible to focus. True to my nature, I found the beep of the cardiac monitor and the intravenous fluid running into my arm reassuring. These were the familiar sights and sounds.

I glanced around the room and thought to myself, *Well, I must still be alive.*

"Anita?"

"What?"

"Did you hear what I just said?"

"Yes, but I think this means I'm going to die."

"It used to mean that, but not any longer. We've made progress. You know, many times people who consume a lot of alcohol get this. Are you sure you don't drink?" She sounded annoyed.

I shook my head.

"And you don't smoke."

"No. I don't smoke." I sighed. "I did. Years ago, when I worked the ER. I used to think it was impossible to be night charge of an ER and not drink gallons of coffee and smoke cigarettes."

She didn't say anything for the moment, and somehow, I felt the need to explain why I'd been a coffee and cigarette junkie. Maybe it was just the drugs talking.

"You know, when you work nights everything in your life is basically turned upside down. I was a single parent and had to get by on very little sleep. So I leaned on cigarettes and coffee. Do you think they made my heart sick? It was so long ago."

Petite Cardiologist looked impatient. "Doubtful," she said. "Your vascular system is fine. It's your heart muscle that's having problems." She paused. "Have you ever been to South America?"

Again I shook my head. "Why are you even asking me about South America?"

"I thought you might have picked up a virus in your travels." She placed several prescriptions on my bedside table. "We'll do a few more blood tests, but for now I want you to get started on these meds. I'm running late, so if you have any problems or questions, just call the office. Otherwise, I'll see you in a week." Already moving toward the door, she added, "I'd like to share the good news with your husband. Is he in the lobby?"

I nodded my stunned, sedated head, and then she was gone.

I was frightened and furious. I thought I had been given a death sentence. I didn't care what Petite Cardiologist had said.

I picked up the prescriptions that had been left at my bedside and attempted to read them. My eyes still couldn't focus. Everything was a blur.

That's when I realized it wasn't just the medication that had made it hard to read the prescriptions. I was crying.

Chapter 3

Side Effects

My cardiac diagnosis tilted my whole world off its axis. It felt like I'd awakened one morning to discover I'd been moved to a new neighborhood in a new city, and I hated it. In fact, it wasn't long before I developed a whole new list of hates.

I hated my new diagnoses: idiopathic cardiomyopathy.

I hated what it made me: a cardiac patient.

But what I hated most of all were the cardiac meds.

Those three little pills the cardiologist had called a "crutch for my heart" had side effects. Big. Fat. Side. Effects.

"Have you read about the side effects? These things are really strong."
I pointed to the three small pills in the palm of my hand.

My husband handed me a glass of water.

I closed my hand and shook my head. "I don't want to take these."

"Please take them." His voice held a slight trace of exasperation. "You can always call the doctor if you have problems."

I gave in and did as he asked. Within an hour of my first dose, the room started to spin.

Here was another hate to add to my HATE LIST: I hated not having a clear head.

It reminded me too much of all the years I struggled as a child to make sense of what was happening around me. My mother drank. My father drank to keep my mother company. Or was it the other way around? I was never sure. In our upscale midwestern neighborhood, everyone drank, often to excess. Liquor seemed to me to be part of every social event. "We're going over to the neighbors for drinks" became code. It meant, "Be on alert. Your parents will come home acting weird. Your mother will be slurring her speech, and your dad will be angry. Everything will upset them, so make yourself scarce."

My headaches started around that time, and I soon found I would become nervous and anxious when issues about my health came up. There was no one I could turn to. Basic childhood diseases were often ignored—or, worse yet, ridiculed.

I had to have a clear head. I needed to think for myself.

Even at ten years of age, I knew I was on my own.

Once I knew the dizziness was here to stay, I phoned the doctor's office and left a message.

The next day, I couldn't catch my breath. Overnight, stairs had become my personal Mt. Everest. I phoned the doctor's office in the morning and again in the afternoon.

When I didn't hear from her by late Friday evening, I knew I wasn't going to hear from her at all.

I fled to the emergency room.

Upon my arrival, the nurses immediately hooked me up to the heart monitor. Within minutes, the ER doctor arrived.

My anxiety was so high I couldn't even wait for him to introduce himself. "I'm a newly diagnosed cardiac patient," I said, "and ever since I've started taking these meds the room never stops spinning. I can't catch my breath. My heart pounds all the time, and my chest hurts. I don't want to take these meds any longer."

"Well, that's quite a story. I'm Dr. Church by the way." He looked up at my heart monitor. "I don't think you'll be able to stop taking them anytime soon." His voice was calm and measured. "Do you have the name and number of your cardiologist?"

I reached into my purse and pulled out her card. "Are you going to call her? I've already tried several times and haven't had any luck."

He smiled and nodded, but that was all. I watched his white coat disappear down the long hallway and then turned my head to stare at the irregular blips on my heart monitor.

Suddenly, in a flash, everything fit.

In a moment of time that passed so fast it would've been difficult to measure, I finally got it. My life was never going to back to normal again.

The thought alone made my chest hurt even more.

It wasn't long before Dr. Church walked back into my room with an air of nonchalance that I found oddly comforting

If I were dying, I thought, *he would've at least come back with a sense of purpose and a couple of nurses in tow.*

"Well," he said, "your doctor and I are in agreement. Stop the meds until you see her next week. Then she'll switch you to something else."

"But," I said with an edge of desperation. "Do I have to take anything?"

"Only if you want to live." His tone left no room for discussion.

My appointment wasn't for another six days. That bought me six days of freedom.

Freedom from rooms that spun and a heart that pounded.

Six days, as it turned out, was just enough time to lull myself into a false sense of maybe.

Maybe, I told myself, *maybe I don't need these meds after all.*

Denial is a hard thing to shake when you don't like the hand you've been dealt.

I began to bargain with God in earnest and soon discovered that it's absolutely amazing how much bargaining you can do when you live in a state of constant desperation.

Over those long six days there were two things I promised God: 1) If You heal me, I will devote my life to missionary work (someplace where the weather isn't too hot and not too far from home would be great); 2) I'd go back into nursing, which, given my age and present condition, I knew was probably a long shot.

I never promised Him my firstborn child because, even under the most extreme circumstances, I knew that was never going to happen. So it was of some comfort to me to know that I did at least have some limits.

My six days of bliss passed all too quickly.

The drive to my next appointment at Petite Cardiologist's office was an exercise in agony.

With each mile that brought us closer to the hospital, tentacles of fear slid out of my heart and spread throughout my chest.

It would have been helpful if someone had told me that cardiac medications can be miracle drugs, but they don't always work. The time frame to find out if they are going to work or not is the same for everyone: six months. None of the meds come without side effects.

I had only three questions I wanted answered that day: 1) Were there other drugs they could give me? 2) Would they work on me? 3) Just how bad were the side effects?

Petite Cardiologist entered the room wearing a smile and spoke first. "The emergency room told me you had a hard time last week. I'm sorry I didn't get a chance to call you back. Last week was very difficult for me."

I sat on the exam table, looking at her. "So, where do we go from here?" I didn't return her smile.

She looked at me, opened up her mouth as if to say something more, and then closed it. When she finally spoke, she sounded annoyed. "Okay, let's try a different combination of drugs to see if things go a little better. I'm taking you off the Coreg and Zestril and placing you on Toprol and Cozaar. However, I do find your reaction to the drugs rather interesting."

I ignored her comment. I didn't even want to know what she meant by interesting. I was focused on the only thing that now mattered to me. "What should I do about the side effects? Everything I've read says they all have side effects."

"The side effects are temporary."

"Well, how long is temporary?"

"That varies for every patient, but you need to stay on the drugs longer than a week. Some of my patients do so well they're able to discontinue taking the meds altogether once their heart has healed."

"Really? Are there many people who get this chance?"

She thought for moment and then said, "Some."

From that moment on, I wanted to be one of the "some." If it had happened to others, why couldn't it happen to me?

I still had one more question to ask: "How will I know if the medication is working?"

"We'll know in six months."

CHAPTER 4

Life in the Temporary Zone

Living life in the Temporary Zone is truly not for the faint of heart. With the dawn of each new day I would look into the mirror, toothbrush in hand, and announce, "The drugs are my friends. Their side effects are only temporary. Today will be better than yesterday."

Repetitive practicing of the mantra actually helped during the day, but mantra or not, it was impossible to ward off the demons of the nighttime.

The pharmacist handed me my new prescriptions with a warning: "You may experience some sleep disturbances."

I didn't question his word of caution, but I should have.

The first sleep disturbance arrived as a full-blown, three-dimensional, in-living-color nightmare. Guns firing. Knives flashing. Cars crashing. The details of the dream remained obscured, but the point was clear: someone wanted me dead, and they were willing to hire a hit squad to get the job done.

The dream woke me up. My nightgown was drenched in sweat.

In the early years of my marriage, nightmares had been frequent visitors to my dream life. Therapy had proven to be helpful, but the childhood trauma I'd suffered as a result of my parents' drinking and abusive behavior continued to leave me vulnerable in nighttime hours.

This present nightmare seemed to be cardiac drug–induced, but whatever the cause, the treatment remained the same.

I slipped out of bed, changed my nightgown, grabbed an extra blanket from the linen closet, and crept downstairs. I turned on the television. I did not care what shows were on at that hour. I would watch anything. Years earlier, I had watched a constant stream of infomercials in an effort to quiet my heart and calm my anxiety. Then products from HSN and QVC began to arrive almost daily at the house, and what had seemed so essential to my life at 2:00 a.m. turned into, "What was I thinking?" with the arrival of each UPS truck.

I returned everything. I even returned (with some sadness) a beautiful set of hand-carved knives that I'd seen cut through a coffee can with a large frozen fish inside. Then I switched to other programming—hoping, if possible, to avoid a repeat of my can't-live-without-it drama from years earlier.

That's when I discovered Bravo TV.

Night after night, while my sleep disturbances raged, the shows of Bravo TV soothed and comforted me. The Housewives of Orange County, Atlanta, and New York quickly became my dead-of-night, super-calming best friends. Their outrageous lives and self-induced problems pulled me through the side effects of my new medications.

Hour after hour, I watched the Housewives. It didn't matter if I'd seen the episodes before. I wasn't watching for entertainment. I was watching to try to feel normal again. The drugs had stolen my sense of normalcy, and I wanted it back.

"The drugs are my friends. Their side effects are only temporary."

The nights dissolved into days. The days dissolved into weeks. The weeks dissolved into months—and finally, when each of the Housewives concluded their respective seasons of hijinx and drama, my night terrors faded.

Still, I continued to wake up in the middle of night. No longer terror stricken, I soon found a new focus for my restlessness: the Internet.

The computer on my desk held me with its laser-like focus. Shards of bright moonbeams poured through the window.

A hand touched my shoulder. I jumped.

"How long have you been up?" my husband asked. Disheveled by sleep, his eyes squinted against the bright light of the screen.

"What time is it?" I whispered.

"3:00 a.m. Why are you whispering?" he asked with a sleepy grin.

I smiled back. "I don't know. I've been up a couple of hours."

"Would you be willing to try and come back to bed?"

I turned away and stared into the darkness outside the window. "I've started to wonder something. Do you think that there's been something about my life story that has literally made my heart sick?"

G blinked. "Do we have to talk about this right now? You need to sleep."

"I don't want to sleep. What if I go to bed and wake up dead in the morning?"

He extended his hand.

I reached for it and followed him down the hallway to our bedroom.

"Just remember," I said as I climbed into bed. "Once I'm dead, I'll have tons of time to sleep."

He patted my hand, reached his arm around my shoulders, and pulled me closer to him. "If you can't sleep, just rest."

His words made me smile. It was what we'd told our grandchildren when they were very young and had told us they were too big to take naps.

⁂

Still, the Internet and I continued to be best buddies. I couldn't let go.

I wanted data. I thought more data equaled better understanding.

Better understanding equaled more control over my situation.

It was all an illusion, of course. Information wasn't going to help me live or die, no matter how much of it I accumulated. I knew that. But researching gave me something to do while the drugs began their healing work.

My present-day drama reminded me of a conversation I'd once had with an ER resident.

"Does the mother really have to go home and give her child a bath even though we've already given him Tylenol?" I asked him. "I mean, it's the middle of the night."

"Yes, she does," he answered with a yawn. "It gives her something to do until the Tylenol has a chance to work."

Chapter 5

Green Bananas

I picked up the phone on the first ring.

It was G.

G is not his real name, of course. His real name is George. I changed it when we first started dating.

He had a tendency to be quite formal in his approach to life, and because it had served him well in business, he didn't see any reason to change it.

In the beginning, I agreed.

However, when his rigid ways spilled over into our relationship, I suggested we shorten his name to G.

"It will help you be more relaxed. Don't you think?"

He stared at me

"Okay," I quickly added. "You look confused, and I don't think you have any idea what I'm talking about, so I'm just going to move ahead with this plan. From now on, you'll be G . . . at least to me."

Twenty years later, I gave him another one of my best smiles when he told me he'd never cared for the fact that I'd changed his name. But after twenty years, he figured "it was too late to do anything about it."

His friends still call him by his given name of George, which makes him happy, but at home he is G, and to all of our eight grandchildren he has become Grandpa G.

It was G who was now calling me on his cell phone from the middle of the produce section of our local grocery store.

"They only have green bananas," he said in a loud whisper.

The panic in his voice caught me off guard. My brain was instantly thrown into problem-solving mode. "Okay," I said. It was the only word that came to mind.

It didn't get us very far.

"I'm telling you they only have green bananas and I don't know what to do," G said in his whisper-shout.

"I know. I heard you. You said they only have green bananas. I just don't understand why that's a problem."

By the time I was diagnosed, G and I had been married for twenty-five years. (Two others preceded him, just in case you were wondering, and for those who believe in such things, the third time has turned out to be the charm.)

G has an unusual gift. If there were honorary degrees given out for such things, he would have his PhD in The Reading of Fine Print.

Once he gathered all the information he needed on my diagnosis from Petite Cardiologist and studied everything he could find on my meds, he drew up a flow sheets and graphs. His conclusion? "Everything is going to be just fine."

So now, when his "we're-going-to-get-through-this-everything-is-going-to-be-just-fine" attitude came to an abrupt halt in the produce section of our local grocery store, I was surprised.

His agitation continued. "What do mean you don't know why

that's a problem? Of course, it's a problem. Now, should I go to another store or not? I don't think I can buy the green ones that are here."

All of a sudden, a switch flipped inside my brain and the light bulb of recognition began to burn. "Aha," I said with great clarity. At last, I knew what the problem was.

Several years earlier, when I'd turned fifty-five, we'd adopted a saying: "We are now living in the no-green-banana zone."

This expression, as we understood it, meant that people of a certain age should only buy ripe bananas, because if you buy green ones you never know if you're going to live long enough to eat them. In the broadest sense, we took the phrase to mean, "If you want to do something, don't put it off. Do it ASAP."

A year later, after he retired, we began in earnest to search for something we could do together that we both enjoyed.

Golf was out. Neither one of us played. We both liked tennis—as long as all we had to do was watch.

Hiking and traveling, however, were definitely in. Success came when we combined the two interests and began to travel with walking groups as a way to see foreign countries.

We tried to pack in as much as we could.

One by one we'd buried our parents, and though we both knew life was finite, we hadn't planned on the fact that finite meant *right now*.

Finite was for other people, not for us.

Which brings me back to my husband's inability to buy the one thing I'd put on the grocery list that morning: bananas.

"Do you think that if you buy green bananas I won't live long enough to eat them?" I asked gently.

G cleared his throat. Several moments passed in silence.

I waited.

Finally, I heard a very soft, "Yes."

Touched by his sudden collapse of ever-present steadiness, I made him a promise:

"Here's what I think you should do. I think you should go ahead and buy the green bananas. If you buy the bananas, I promise I will live long enough to eat them."

Again, the long pause.

"I love you," I reassured him. "I'm sorry this is so hard."

Again, I heard him clear his throat. And then: "Thank you."

Several days passed before I fully understood just how frightened my husband had been that day in the produce section. My cardiac diagnosis had unhinged him.

He'd never shown how he felt, and until now, I'd never known.

I don't think he'd even known himself.

It wasn't until he came face to face with the dreaded green bananas in the produce section of our local grocery store that he realized something he hadn't wanted to acknowledge before: living in the no-green-bananas zone had become very scary business.

Chapter 6

Well, That's Just Plain Crazy

I was tired of being scared and depressed. It was wearing me out. I wanted to work on acceptance of my diagnosis and treatment, but I lived in a small, rural town where support groups for patients with heart disease were nonexistent. So I went back to see what my new BFF, the Internet, had to say about all things cardiac.

I was particularly curious about what the web had to say about my new drugs. A handful of side effects were consistently mentioned on several different sites: "Cardiac medications can and often do produce depression and fatigue. Tell your physician if symptoms persist."

What was my response to this newfound information? I did nothing. I did have a thought, however: *Maybe I should mention this the next time I see the doctor.*

My visits to Petite Cardiologist's office were now routine. "So, how's your walking going?" she asked while checking my pulse.

I hesitated. "My walking? Oh, my walking is going okay."

She listened to my lungs, then probed for more information. "What does okay mean?"

"Oh, about forty-five minutes a day." The tone in her voice made me uneasy. Something was up.

"The Japanese have done studies," she said. "They've indicated that ten thousand steps a day is what you need to become heart beneficial. So, get yourself a pedometer and check in with me by email before your next visit."

"Ten thousand steps!" I repeated, eyes wide. "Well, that's just plain crazy. I might as well throw in the towel right here and now, because there is no way I'm never going to be able to walk ten thousand steps a day. I mean, I did an Avon Walk five years ago and walked sixty miles in three days, but that was for charity and it wasn't easy. I lost three of my toenails and couldn't walk for a week after I got home because my feet were so swollen."

I turned to G, who was sitting in the corner of the room looking somewhat amused.

"Do *you* think I can do ten thousand steps a day?"

"I think we can try," he said.

By the time I left the office, I felt overwhelmed. All I could think about was that Japanese study. I didn't tell Petite Cardiologist how depressed I was. I already knew what she'd say: "Well, you know everything is only temporary. Tell me if it becomes more severe and we'll give you something for it."

I didn't want any more drugs. I wasn't going to take one more pill. No matter how bad it got.

CHAPTER 7

And We're Walking

Greater love hath no man than my husband for all data that can be measured, charted, or graphed.

Within twenty-four hours of our visit to the doctor's office, he'd purchased me a brand-new, bright blue pedometer. I quickly discovered that unless we started every morning with a five-mile walk, the ten thousand steps remained just some number from a study conducted in a Japanese doctor's research lab.

Early morning turned out to be the best time to walk. If we waited, the heat of the day activated another dreaded medication side effect: nausea. The greater the heat, the worse the nausea.

"What makes those Japanese think they're so smart,anyway?" I asked G on mile number three of our early-morning walk.

"The Japanese are smart folks." G loves smart people.

"I know the Japanese are smart people." I held up my hand. "Can we stop and rest for moment? I can't talk and walk at the same time. I get too out of breath." I leaned over and placed both my hands on top of my thighs.

G touched my back. "Are you okay?"

"Three times already you've asked me that question," I said sourly. "I'm fine. I just need to stop for moment. My heart is pounding. These hills are hard, and I'm not even convinced that these guys who ran this study ever tried to walk with half their heart in failure."

G launched into a minor discourse on how these studies are usually conducted, and how even though he hadn't read everything he needed to know on this study, he was sure the Japanese knew what they were talking about.

Still bent over, I sucked air and tried to get G to see my point of view. "TMI, G. TMI."

I stood up and stared at the road ahead. "I'm really tired. You don't suppose . . ."

I would love to tell you that G had sympathy for my plight and offered to go get the car. He did not.

"I will walk with you, but I won't carry you." He put his arm around my shoulder and urged me onward. "My job is to encourage you and not give in. We still have trips to take."

The hill before us began to melt away.

"All you need is one more mile," G said cheerfully.

He needed me, he told me, to be travel-ready. He reminded me that we traveled well together, and that walking used to be one of the things we did best.

"Africa is waiting," he said. "And Greece. Remember how much you loved Greece?"

"Florence," I said. "Isn't Florence waiting?"

Banter is a game we play.

"Hmm, yes," he said, now out of breath himself. "Wait a minute. We've already seen a lot of Italy. How about more of Spain?"

"Spain? Spain sounds good. Remember the night we heard Fado

music in Barcelona for the first time, and we felt like idiots because we'd arrived so early at the restaurant for dinner?"

"I still don't think that 9:00 p.m. is too early for dinner," G said, exasperation in his tone. His stomach is happiest when Western rules of eating are in effect.

"Next time we'll remember to go later . . . if there is a next time."

"There will be a next time," G reassured me.

And, we're walking . . .

CHAPTER 8

Just Ask Barbra Streisand

Insomnia continued to plague my late-night hours.
I simply could not shake the feeling that one morning I was going
to wake up dead.

Night and day, the computer remained my constant comforter
and friend. Yes, I wanted answers to questions about heart disease,
but that wasn't the only gift the computer gave me.

The land of Facebook soon added endless hours of distraction. I
looked up old lovers and former friends.

I questioned everything.

Had the life I'd led contributed to my heart disease diagnosis?
Had there been too many divorces? Too many men? Had my parents
been too abusive? For most of my adult life, I'd been a single parent.
Had all the years of my hard work in the end been too hard and the
years too many?

Lots of questions. Not so many answers.

"You're obsessed," G said one morning at breakfast. "How late
were you up last night? I'm not angry. Just curious."

I ignored his question and denied his observation. "I don't think I'm obsessed."

"Well, what would you call it?" he pressed.

"Ruminating. I'm ruminating and learning things. For instance, did you know that somewhere in this world a woman dies every minute from heart disease? It outranks cancer as the number one reason women die. Just ask Barbara Streisand if you don't believe me."

"Isn't ruminating something cows do? And what does Barbara Streisand have to do with anything?"

"She happens to be dedicated to raising awareness of cardiac disease in women and has a whole center named after her at Cedars-Sinai Hospital. And I have no idea if cows ruminate or not."

"Okay." He sounded unconvinced.

"Okay what?"

"Just okay." He shrugged. "You're still spending an awful lot of time at that computer."

Call it ruminating or call it obsessing, my life as a cardiac patient had turned into a full-time job.

The second round of cardiac drugs had started to improve my life. The shortness of breath had disappeared, and along with it the rooms that spun every time I stood up.

My depression had begun to lift slightly, and there were moments when I dared to hope. Would I be one of the lucky ones who could live with a dying heart?

And that's when it happened. Right in the middle of the first moment of confidence I'd had in almost three months. My heart flipped a somersault inside my chest.

Cardiac gymnastics from irregular heartbeats had become part of my daily routine, but I'd never felt it like this.

This one was like a full-out somersault off the uneven parallel bars.

This was the kind of thud that makes your eyes bug out of your head.

My brain immediately launched into its Post-it note routine: *Breathe. Okay, now breathe again. Good. Now go to the phone. Good. Now pick it up. Now call your doctor.*

Petite Cardiologist was calm in response to my report of my heart's gymnastics.

"Oh, those are called PVCs—premature ventricular contractions," she said. "They're heartbeats that occur outside the normal electrical circuit. We don't worry about them unless they start to become more frequent. If that happens, we might want to consider putting in a pacemaker. Patients with your low heart function are at higher risk for sudden death."

Now this I found absolutely astonishing. "Sudden death? Did you just say *sudden death*?" The Post-it notes started coming faster and faster. *Don't worry. You'll be fine. Keep talking. Keep breathing.*

"That's correct. There's nothing to worry about right now. You are really going to be fine. I'd ask you come to the hospital if I thought you were at any risk. Call me if they increase in number; otherwise, we'll wait until your next appointment."

She sounded done with the conversation, but I pressed her for more. "If they do put in a pacemaker, isn't that considered surgery?"

"We don't like to think of it in those terms. Pacemakers are done in the Special Procedure Room, but I think we're getting ahead of ourselves. Let's just see where we are at the next appointment."

I hung up the phone and stared at the framed pictures of my grandchildren scattered throughout the living room. I'd added so many photos since my diagnosis that G had begun calling the living room "Anita's picture farm."

But I needed all of them, and more. The pictures had the power to calm me whenever my heart decided to take a spontaneous flying leap off the Empire State Building.

I sat on the sofa, gazed over my farm, and started to smile. An old family memory floated up through my present-day cardiac haze.

Three girls and one bathroom is a guaranteed source of conflict for any family, and ours was no exception. Mornings on any given school day often ended in disaster.

My older sister, Char, the cheerleader and soon-to-be Summer Festival Princess, had, as usual, exceeded her time limit in the bathroom.

I wanted her out.

I pounded on the bathroom door. "Are you coming out anytime soon?"

Char ignored my pleas.

I pounded on the door harder and screamed, "Will you PLEASE get out of the bathroom?

My act of desperation provoked her even more. "Go away," she shouted. "I hate you. Why can't you leave me alone? You're such a little pest. Why don't you just take a flying leap off the Empire State Building?"

"No," I yelled back. "Why don't *you* take a flying leap!?"

Hardly an original response, but effective. Moments later, she marched out with hairbrush in hand and her overstuffed makeup bag clutched to her chest. The smell of Aqua Net hair spray filled the hallway.

I got up from the sofa, overwhelmed by a sense of longing. I wanted to call my sister and tell her I finally knew what it felt like to take that flying leap—but when was the last time we had talked? Years, maybe?

Over time, we'd drifted apart. We'd had a difficult relationship with no easy way back.

How, I wondered, do you start a conversation with a sister who's simply drifted away?

Rilke, the German poet, once wrote, "Our lives are shaped by those who love us and those who do not."

I found the quote printed on a card when I was a young nursing student in search of answers to life's big questions. Rilke's words stayed with me.

Perhaps the time had come to give equal gratitude for those who'd loved me and those who hadn't. Even if the person in my family who had not loved me the most turned out to be my mother.

CHAPTER 9

Heart Sick

Not long ago, I'd read in an article online that when a pregnant mother's diet is insufficient, the developing fetus will cull all the nutrients he or she needs from the mother's teeth and bone.

Women are built to be selfless.

I wondered: Could the same be true of my heart?

Left to fend for itself through years of overwork and lack of care, had my heart culled all it could from my body and ultimately outsourced the job of staying alive to the cardiac medications?

I am a woman who loves order. My ancestors were German. Few things please me more than a clean house. Control lives in my DNA, and my cardiac diagnosis was not part of the plan for my life.

Desperate to gain some control over my new life, I decided to forge ahead with a new plan.

The first part of the plan was difficult but already in place: acceptance of my diagnoses. I didn't think the second part wasn't going to be any easier than the first, but I wanted to try.

If I was going to be a cardiac patient for the rest of my life, which it seemed that I was, then I wanted to try to gain a new understanding of my life's story.

Was there a possibility, I wondered, that my experiences had literally made my heart sick?

CHAPTER 10

Everybody Has a Mother

Every year on my birthday, my mother told me the same story: "No one ever cared about you on the night you were born, you know. The country was at war. Dad was in Italy. Everyone cared about him, of course, but you? 'Call me when it's over' was all your grandmother had to say to me when I went into labor.

"Six weeks after you were born," she went on, "your entire body burned up with a fever and it just wouldn't go away. I was so terrified. I thought you were going to die. So I drove all night from Minneapolis with you and your sister clear up to that small Catholic hospital near the Canadian border close to where your grandpa and grandma lived. Those nuns saved you, you know. They were simply wonderful. Never disappointed me. I almost became a convert right then and there. I was so grateful to them."

The nuns may have not have disappointed her, but the doctors gave her little reason to hope. "Your daughter has an infection in the bone," they told her. "It's called osteomyelitis. We have no cure for this. You must prepare yourself for the worst."

The year was 1943, and even though penicillin had experienced great success in the military, it was still being used only on a limited basis in the general population.

No one knew the answer to the question that was on everyone's mind: would penicillin work on an infant with an infection in the bone?

Someone needed to make a decision.

My mother begged the Mother Superior. "Try. Please try."

Three days later, a small twin-engine plane landed in a frozen field that doubled as a landing strip. The penicillin was on board.

The dosage and administration of the drug was all guesswork. I received millions of units around the clock and continued to receive penicillin injections every month for the first five years of my life.

I've often thought that the seeds of my mother's discontent were sown in those early weeks of my life, for our relationship remained forever tense. A simple request for food when I was hungry would cause her to shake her head and sigh with exasperation. My occasional requests for school clothes from elementary school onward were ignored.

Ask her on a good day and she'd mutter, "You've always been so much work."

Ask her on a bad day and she would add, "You know, you would have died if it wasn't for me."

The fact that I lived when I should have died was the only gift she was able to give me, and in her mind that gift should be enough.

Whatever the reason, one thing was clear, at least to me: my mother did not love me.

It is a painful fact to admit even now that I am old and she has been dead for several years, but at least it gives me comfort, albeit of the somewhat cold variety, to know that there was nothing I could've done to change what happened.

CHAPTER 11

Stealth of a Serpent

Throughout my childhood I was obsessed with my mother's hands, but after all the destruction they caused, how could it have been otherwise?

The slightest infraction of childhood misbehavior would open the floodgates to a reign of terror. Torn and dirty playclothes were enough to send her into a mad frenzy of hitting from which there was no escape. No one in the family—not my beautiful older sister, not my brilliant younger sister, not even my cherished younger brother— was exempt from her hands, which could move with the stealth of a serpent and strike with terrifying speed.

My mother and her dry, chapped, nail-bitten hands were never at rest.

My sister once told me, "When Mother wrings her hands, it sounds like someone's scraping paint off a wall with sandpaper. I don't even have to see her. The moment I hear that sound, I know: Mother has entered the room."

I inherited my mother's German, sturdy, best-used-for-working-in-the-fields hands and have always felt that they were ugly. So ugly, in fact, that when I was younger I refused to shake hands with adults for fear they would discover what I had identified as my personal shame.

However, one year while traveling through a deeply snow-covered Germany, I discovered something about my heritage that freed me from the bondage of my memory and gave me the gift of understanding.

It happened in Dresden. My husband and I were eating in a restaurant that looked, with its warm, dark wood, long family-style dining tables, and artificial gas lights, like the essence of a German hunting lodge.

We had arrived without reservations and the only places left were at the end of a table big enough for eight that already contained five seated dinner guests. When it became apparent that two of the expected party had canceled, we were given their seats.

We hadn't been seated long when the sixth and last member of their party arrived.

Without hesitation and with great enthusiasm, this heavy-set, middle-aged late arrival introduced herself to us, first reaching for my hand and booming out *"Guten Abend!"* then rushing around the table, pumping G's hand, and again announcing, *"Guten Abend!"*

Glasses were raised all around and a party atmosphere began to fill the room.

I leaned toward my husband and whispered over their laughter, "She has hands like my mother . . . only different."

He looked puzzled. "Different?"

I thought for a moment and then said, "Her hands are kind."

Physically, of course, my hands still look the same way they always have—but to me they are not the same. Now when I look at my hands, instead of seeing my mother I see a nameless German woman who reached for my hand and freed me from a lifetime of pain and sorrow—who gently gave me the gift of understanding.

My heart, at last, was beginning to comprehend what my head had rejected for years:

Love would not come to me from the people I'd wanted to love me the most. It might, however, catch me unaware and warm me on a cold and snowy night in Germany through the strength of a stranger's handshake.

A door to understanding had cracked open—but where was it going to lead me?

Chapter 12

Real Snappy Dresser

Once you have been diagnosed with a potentially fatal heart disease, doctors become very interested in your parents.

"So," my internist asked, "how old were your parents when they died?"

"They were both eighty," I said. "They died three weeks apart."

"Hmm, and what was the cause of death?"

"Heart attacks."

"Both of them?"

I nodded.

"Interesting . . . Don't you think?"

I shrugged. "Actually, the interesting part came way before they died."

"In what way?"

I paused for a second. I'd known my internist for over thirty years, but until now I'd never really needed her for anything too serious. I'd made this appointment to see her, however, because I wanted more information. True, I had a cardiologist, but I wanted someone who knew *me*, not just my clinical heart.

My doctor looked at me but said nothing.

I'd come to ask her a specific question, and now that the time had arrived, and I couldn't do it. I felt stuck. An old tape began to play in my head—the voice of my therapist from a long time ago. It was part of the reason I was in the internist's office today.

"That's it?" The therapist had a quizzical look on his face. "That's all you can say? I ask you to describe your relationship with your father and all you can say is, 'He's a real snappy dresser?'"

"Look," I said, more frustrated than mad, "I don't want to talk about him at all. You're the one who keeps bringing him up. I haven't seen my dad in over ten years, and what's more I don't intend to see him anytime soon."

The therapist extended his long, thin fingers and tapped them together. "Do you remember the diagnostic tests I gave you when you first came here?"

"Yes." I stared down at the Kleenex in my lap.

"Well, the results from those tests show that you have issues with your father that might need some work."

"Issues? What kind of issues?"

"Why don't you tell me a little more about this real snappy dresser, and maybe we can find out together what the issues might be."

I dropped my head further. I couldn't look at him. I already knew what the issues were. Finally, I raised my head. "My dad is totally messed up. "

The therapist said nothing

I looked down at my Kleenex and watched the tears fall, drop by drop, into my lap.

"I'm not going to talk about what my dad did. Not now. Not ever.

He beat me once. Blackened my eye and left me with a swollen lip because I greeted my boyfriend with a kiss at the airport. He said, 'The airport is a public place and you have disgraced the family with your behavior.' Both of my parents were big on humiliation. So, no. I'm not going to talk about him, today or any other time. You can tell me whatever you want about what those stupid tests showed, and I'll tell you you're 100 percent correct, but it won't change my mind about talking. I'll talk about my mother, but I'm not talking about my dad."

Again, the therapist said nothing. Several seconds later, he cleared his throat and asked, "How do you expect me to help you if you won't talk?"

"I didn't say that. I said I wasn't going to talk about my dad. He's the only thing I won't talk about. And as far as how you're going to help me? That's your job. You're the one who's the doctor here. Not me."

"Can I ask you one question about him?"

"Sure, but I may not answer it."

"How do you feel about your dad now?"

Tears broke through the dam of my reserve. I reached for more Kleenex. "Broken-hearted. Whenever I think of my dad, it feels like someone has taken a baseball bat to my heart and smashed it in two."

"Anita? . . . Are you here with me?"

My internist was staring at me.

I smiled. "Yes. I guess you caught me daydreaming. Actually, I came here today to ask you a question about my diagnosis."

"Don't you think you should ask your cardiologist?"

I looked down at my lap. "I can't talk to her. Besides, it's sort of a weird question. "

"What is it?"

"Well, it's something that I've been thinking about a lot lately. Do you think that if a person is abused as a child, the effects of the abuse can lay low for, say . . . years, and then one day everything will surface and make the person really sick?"

"Were you abused?"

"Yes."

"For how long?"

"Years. I've already had tons of therapy for it. I just want to know—as a physician, do you think an abusive childhood made my heart sick?"

Her brow furrowed. "It's hard to say. As a medical professional, I tend to look for answers founded in the clinical data. The nature of your heart diagnosis suggests you picked up a virus somewhere in your travels."

I liked this woman. She was smart and kind. She was also a traditionalist.

"However," she went on, "it's hard to rule out any of the contributing factors. Whatever they might be. The important thing is, everyone in this office wants you well. So, stay on your meds—they seem to be working—and let's see you in three months."

Maybe she was right about the clinical data, but she'd left the dooropen to a possibility. I wanted to go back.

Had my family-related heartaches left footprints on my heart?

Chapter 13

Starry, Starry Night

The stars in the winter sky dazzled in their brilliance and abundance. The night air was sharp and cold. Mounds of winter snow from a recent storm were piled high by the side of the road, and another storm was on its way. Tall pine trees glistened in the open field across the street. Shards of light cast off by the moon danced on their branches. We walked together, hand in hand, through the winter wonderland, listening to the snow crunch under our feet, unaware that this would be our last Christmas together.

Earlier that evening, he'd surprised me with a knock at the door. A Christmas present was tucked underneath his arm; he asked if we could go for a walk. He was sixteen. I was seventeen. It was 1960 and we were both in crazy, mad, teenage love.

His love for me was a gift in ways he never could have imagined.

He'd been born into a socially successful, over-achieving family— a family typical of our upper-middle-class community. My family, in contrast, reeked of alcohol, abuse, and dysfunction.

It was a secret I'd kept from the world. The facts of my life were too painful to admit even to myself. The fact that, for instance, my mother barely functioned through the fog of an alcoholic haze and often, whenever the fog temporarily cleared, declared how much she hated me.

My existence alone irritated my mother daily—but nothing enraged her more than my newfound romance. She seethed in anger every time I attended a school dance. Arbitrary, unreasonable curfews ruled my entire dating life.

And Christmas holidays in our household were an especially dangerous time. They could bring out the worst in my mother. So my boyfriend's knock at the door on that cold winter night promised potential heartbreak for me.

I knew I had to ask for permission to leave the house. If I didn't ask and I went without her permission, there would be no rest for me when I returned.

I found my mother sitting on the sofa, staring with unfocused eyes in the direction of the door. The drink she'd been nursing remained on the kitchen counter. She'd heard the knock. She'd heard his request.

And so I asked. And I waited. And waited.

Finally, her answer came. "Fine. Just go." She said this with a dismissive wave of her hand.

Bundled up for winter, we opened the door, dashed down the front steps, and quickly headed over to an isolated, snow-covered bench across the street.

"Was your mom okay?" he asked with genuine concern.

I smiled. "She's fine. I think she just had one of her migraines or something."

He stared at me for a second. "You sure?"

I flashed an even bigger smile. "Yes. I'm sure."

He searched my face with mild suspicion and then, with little fanfare, reached down to his lap and handed me his gift.

I took my gloves off and let my fingers linger over the royal blue box. The name of the store it had come from, known for fashion and elegance, was scrolled in silver in the corner. The silver metallic bow on top was the perfect accent.

The box was so beautiful there was no need for wrapping paper. I was relieved. The severe cold had brought pain to my gloveless hands the moment I stepped outside. It would've made opening the present difficult.

I removed the top of the box and stared inside.

Hidden under layers of royal blue tissue paper was a scarf. A long, white, sheer silk scarf. It was delicate and feminine. A symbol of everything I believed I wasn't.

I loved it.

"Do you want to put it on?" He sounded tentative.

With great tenderness and caution, I slipped it over my head. When I began to tie it under my chin, he stopped me.

"No. No." He laughed. "Just wrap it and let it fall on your shoulders. It's supposed to be pretty. Not very useful, I guess."

I did as he asked. I felt awkward. I felt clumsy. I felt loved.

"Perfect," he whispered as he took me in his arms. "It's perfect."

We got up and began to walk down the road.

Snowflakes had started to drift down from the sky. In the distance, a neighbor's dog barked.

This was the world we had created, and in our world, I felt safe, and loved, and protected.

❧

His parents announced in early spring that they would be spending the entire summer in Europe.

It was to be a family trip. He was expected to go.

My mother greeted the news with glee when I told her.

"Good. At last it's over. Now maybe you'll be able to get a job and earn some money this summer. It's time you thought about how you're going to help us pay for your nurse's training in the fall. You certainly can't expect us to do it all."

But it wasn't over. It would take years for it to be really, truly over. Because I never forgot the about scarf, or the boy who gave it to me. With every move, with every transition I made further and further into adult life, I packed and unpacked the scarf. And I continued to wear it until it became yellow and frayed with age.

With every move, I also remembered. I remembered a night in December when a sixteen-year-old boy named Peter came to my door and gave me a gift, and a memory that lasted a lifetime.

CHAPTER 14

For the Love of Tropical Fish
(A Brief Story from a Brief Marriage)

Garrett, my husband-at-the-time, just loved fish. Not ones with good, strong, masculine names like bass, trout, and walleye—no, he liked the tropical fish with lyrical names like clown, star, and yellow tang.

I never really cared one way or the other about how many fish he wanted or how many tanks he needed to accommodate his ever-growing passion. And I never concerned myself with the how much his hobby cost or how he cared for his small army of rare saltwater creatures. I left all of that up to him and his accountants.

The only reason I mention any of this is because you need to understand why I was in such a state of surprise when two IRS auditors showed up at our door one day.

"We're here to ask your husband some questions."

Now this got my attention. I was curious, and just a little bit frightened. (Our newly minted marriage had been difficult from the start.)

"About?"

"His tax returns. Is he home? I think he's expecting us."

"But he has accountants who handle all of that."

"We'd like to talk to your husband about his tropical fish."

"His fish?"

"His fish."

And why, you might ask, was the IRS so curious about my husband's fish?

It's a good question. I asked the same thing myself, and here is the answer (at least, here is the answer my successful, brilliant, gifted, OB-GYN husband-at-the-time gave on that day): "It's all for my patients," he said with an air of great authority and mild condescension.

When the men from the IRS looked doubtful, my husband redoubled his efforts to look more confident. In the process, he also appeared more condescending.

Even I could tell that condescension wasn't an effective strategy with these two men.

"You have to understand," he continued. "When patients visit my office, they are often anxious. Studies have shown that saltwater fish have the ability to soothe and calm.

Based on these findings, I feel the deductions and all attendant services I've taken on the two large saltwater aquariums in my waiting room are justified."

The auditors appeared unmoved. They continued to thumb their way through the pages of his tax returns.

Finally, one of them cleared his throat. "It was second graders," he said.

Garrett looked perplexed. "Pardon me?"

The agent looked up. "The study was done on second graders, not expectant mothers. They found that when second graders had a fish tank in their room, they scored better on their achievement exams. But you know something, Doc?"

I saw Garrett's nostrils flare. He hated being called "Doc."

"They concluded it was the hum of the motor the kids liked. Can you believe it? It was actually the hum of the water purifier that made the kids do better. I guess it was like white noise or something."

The inevitable silence of the damned filled the room before the second auditor weighed in.

"Pets are considered a luxury item. We are not going to allow you to take your fish as a deduction, and furthermore we'd like to see all of your books for the last three years."

In hindsight, I now see that it was on that very day, that exact moment in time, when the bell began to toll for our marriage.

My husband did not like to be challenged.

Nor did he care to have his entire lifestyle downsized, which is exactly what happened after the IRS was finished with him.

Gone were the fish tanks. Gone were the ski trips to Aspen, cruises to the Caribbean, and his new red Porsche. And, after several months of therapy, gone was the marriage.

"I need to make a fresh start," he said to the therapist on what turned out to be our last visit together. "A whole new beginning."

The following week, he stunned me by moving out and doing just exactly that.

One year later, when our marriage was officially over, he called to tell me he was getting married again.

I was not surprised. I'd already heard through friends that he'd acquired a new girlfriend, soon—very soon—after he'd announced to me that he wanted to start his "whole new beginning."

I managed to tell him I wished him well, which at the time was only sort of true.

Intrigued by the thought of his soon-to-be new wife, I took our final moments together on the phone to address an issue I thought was important.

"Could I ask you question?

"Hmm . . ."

"This woman?"

"Yes?" He sounded guarded.

"How much does she like fish?"

Chapter 15

Surprised by Death
(Another Marriage, Another Time)

The last time I saw him, he lay in a hospital bed dying.

By the time he had been diagnosed, several years had passed since our divorce, and I had been reluctant to go see him.

When his doctor called me early that morning to say that they needed a Do Not Resuscitate Order, I told him, "Call his girlfriend."

The doctor's response stunned me: "He told us he wanted you."

It was pancreatic cancer. By the time I arrived at his bedside, obstructive jaundice had turned his body an intense lime-green.

Surrounded by the bleached whiteness of hospital sheets, his arms and face appeared to give off an almost incandescent glow.

It was heart-wrenching to see his body, once so filled with life, now diseased and dying.

When he spoke, he spoke only of regret and wanting another chance at life.

"There are so many things I would've done differently," he said in a voice so weak I had to strain to hear it. "So many things . . ."

I reached for his hand and was shocked to see that he still wore his wedding band. I'd taken mine off years earlier.

In the early years of our marriage, convinced that God had brought us together, we wrapped ourselves in a cocooned state of love and adoration.

The arrival of children sealed our love, but unwittingly ushered in our doom. What he craved—the constant affection and adoration of his congregation (which at times numbered in the thousands)—the girls and I were unable to give him. What the children needed, his time and attention, he either couldn't or didn't want to give.

The marriage unraveled slowly and with great pain. At the time, his position of leadership in the Baptist church made divorce all but impossible.

In the end, after I publicly accepted the blame for all that had gone wrong with our marriage, he retained his position and I was set free.

Get-well cards were stacked high upon the bedside table. Many of them came from concerned members of the church. Others were from people high in ecclesiastical circles. When I remarked upon the abundance of well-wishers, he barely nodded his head in response.

He'd always sought fame through his music in the world. God

had given him fame through his music in the church. It was a gift he never wanted. A blessing he was never able to receive.

Overwhelmed with sadness, I sat at his bedside and wept. I was surprised to find him so ill that he might actually die, and yet, two days later, that's exactly what he did.

More than 1,200 people attended his funeral, but I sat alone in my grief, and was surprised by the depth of my sorrow. I thought all my grieving had ended when the marriage unraveled.

If someone had told me that I would suffer such profound despair at his passing, I would never have believed them. I didn't think women grieved over their ex-husbands, and even if they did I certainly didn't expect to grieve over mine. There had been too many years filled with anger and pain. Too few filled with forgiveness and love.

But in the weeks and months that followed his funeral, I came to a realization that brought me to new understanding. I'd forgotten how much I used to love this man. I'd forgotten because our love had existed years earlier, in another time, another place—another life. I also came to understand that my grief was for that very love, which had died many years earlier.

My pain was for a lifetime of worn-out hopes. My sadness was for all our dreams—dreams that had burned with such a white-hot intensity when we were young.

Dreams that, although they had been packed away, my heart remembered . . . still.

Chapter 16

And Then There Were Others

Married and divorced twice by the time I was thirty-three, I decided to give up on romance and keep my life buried under the stressors of raising two young children. Given my less-than-stellar marital track record I wasn't exactly looking for a new relationship, but then again, I wasn't exactly *not* looking, either.

In the deep recesses of my brain—and heart—I still thought that The One existed. Somewhere. Out there.

I also thought that because I had been raised in a violent, dysfunctional family, I'd seen and heard everything there was to see and hear. Convinced that I could handle anything that came my way, I completely discounted what was most often said about me at the time—that I was naive in the extreme.

I understood why people believed this to be true, of course. I didn't drink. I'd never tried drugs. I regularly attended church and sang in the church choir. Most of the jokes that contained sexual innuendos and were tossed about during the late-night and early-morning hours at the hospital were lost on me.

I worked constantly to support my girls, and because the night shift continued to pay the greatest hourly wage, I tried to pick up as many of those shifts as possible for extra overtime pay.

The big negative: I was horrifically sleep deprived. The big positive: I liked the fast pace of the emergency room and found working with the ever-changing ER residents who staffed the department fun and challenging. I also liked the people who worked nights. The symbiosis of the staff was palpable. Everybody needed each other. Everyone, doctors included, worked together.

We felt we were competent and confident, and even though the nature of work was stressful, we all knew we could count on each other. We all were also on a first-name basis with almost everyone who worked the night shift.

Our doctors rotated through the department on a nightly basis. David showed up in the normal rotation of residents, and in the beginning, there was nothing about our relationship that suggested we would ever be anything but professional. Did I find him attractive? Yes. But no more so than many of the physicians I had worked with over the years. He did have a rapid-fire sense of humor, but that, in my book, equaled fun—not serious. Still, as the months wore on I found myself checking the resident schedule with greater frequency and interest. I was always looking for David's name.

The night we finally worked together again we were swamped with nonstop cases. First came the car accident, then the gunshot wound, and on and on. All night long we worked, talked, ate, and drank coffee. The night went well. The patients got better, and David and I clicked as a team. When morning came, he asked me out. Did I want to go with him to a friend's wedding in Half Moon Bay? Without hesitation, I said yes.

The wedding upended my tentative feelings. I was delighted to find his friends so welcoming. When they teased him about being an adrenaline junkie, I laughed.

I knew what that felt like. I got my adrenaline fix by working in the emergency room. David got his from black diamond runs at the Whistler Ski Resort in Canada.

Their conversations that afternoon, so ordinary to them, were seductive and exciting to me. My life paled in comparison. I'd never even heard of Whistler, let alone known of anyone who had skied there.

Several of the wedding guests knew each other. They'd all met as undergrads at Stanford. David was no exception.

The reception dwindled down until just a few of us were left, and as the afternoon drifted into the early evening, social dates were set for future tennis matches in the city. David loved tennis.

When I told him I'd never played, he responded with infectious enthusiasm. "Oh, you've got to learn. I'll teach you!"

We left the wedding in his vintage dark green Mustang convertible and headed out toward Highway 1. The sky was filled with sinking sunlight. The musty scent of the ocean hovered in the air.

"My friends really liked you," David shouted over the noise of the wind, smiling.

I tried to keep my hair from swamping my face and shouted back, "I liked them too!"

He reached for my hand and kissed my fingertips. A long-forgotten feeling I barely remembered made its intense presence known when he said with a smile, "It's all good. Really good."

The feeling was desire.

I returned to work that night convinced that a whole new world had just opened up.

Had I finally met The One?

It wasn't easy for me to establish a dating life. Between raising the girls and work, I had very little time left for anything else, and David's life was complicated as well. He was both working in the Emergency Department at our hospital and completing his last year of residency at his primary hospital. But we saw each other whenever we could, and we spoke on the phone often. He never spent the night at my place and it was rare when for me to spend a night at his, but when we did, our time together was entertaining and intensely physical. He was talented, athletic, and adventurous. He made life fun.

Soon, perhaps too soon, we began to talk about a future together.

When he suggested he meet the girls, I was surprised by my reluctance.

"Can't we just wait?" I asked. "They've been through so much."

He looked disheartened by my response. "But we're going to be a family some day and I know how important they are to you."

I nodded. "In time." I was nervous. Why was I nervous?

And then a curious thing began to happen. The longer we dated, the more reserved David became. He was still charming and attentive, but definitely quieter.

Eventually, he told me he was going to therapy for a broken engagement and some of the sessions were difficult. He was also quick to reassure me, "I'm getting a handle on it."

I chose to believe him. I had crossed over. I wanted this to work out.

And then, quite suddenly, he dropped out of sight for two weeks. He continued to call to reassure me that he was simply overwhelmed by work.

I knew that residents were famously overworked. I was concerned, but that was all. No alarm bells went off. Not one. Not even the faintest ringing of a little jingle bell.

His last call came to me while I was on duty at 1:30 a.m. His voice was subdued in the extreme.

"Is something wrong?" I asked.

"I'm just discouraged. Are you busy? I have something I want to tell you. If you don't have any patients, I'll drive over to the hospital and park in the corner of the parking lot."

I was thrilled with his phone call but surprised he was up so late on one of his only nights off. "Our last patient left ten minutes ago," I said. "This is such a happy surprise!"

"Great. I'll see you in ten minutes."

I hung up the phone and opened the glass door of the emergency room.

A light fog had rolled in. The overhead lights in the parking lot burned low through the night mist into the few parked cars that remained. A prickly sensation suddenly began to move up my arms.

I turned to the night secretary. "I'm sort of nervous. It looks creepy out there."

But all of my fears became only whispers of concern when I saw his green Mustang pull into the driveway.

I ran to his car and pulled open the passenger side door—and the person I saw behind the steering wheel stunned me. My eyes couldn't register it. My brain couldn't comprehend it. It felt like I'd impaled my heart on a sword. I simply did not know what I was looking at.

Was it David in a clown costume? Or was it David dressed in someone else's clothes?

And if it was David, why was he wearing a dress? And what had happened to his scruffy beard that I loved so much? Fear bordering on terror struck me speechless.

Neither one of us moved. He stayed frozen in the driver's seat. He was wearing a flower-printed dress and a long, frosted blond wig styled in a '60s flip. His bright pink blusher, which would've looked better on life-sized County Fair doll, paled in comparison to his well-defined red lipstick.

Who was this person?

"This," he said, "is what I've been trying to tell you."

When he reached for me with his hand, his college class ring—the one I'd so often admired—caught a glint of light streaming down from an overhead street lamp.

My knees buckled. I dropped to the ground. When I heard the car door click shut behind me, I knew that our dreams for the future had just exploded into the night air.

Seconds later I jumped up to my feet and started to run. Back to the lights of the ER. Back to antiseptic smells and safety of the hospital.

Back to the comfort of IV fluids, gurneys, bandages, and back-boards. Back to the nurses who would support me through the night and in the days to come. My body shook.

No matter how many warm blankets they wrapped around me, I couldn't stop shaking. I tried to talk, but my teeth chattered so hard I couldn't get my mouth to form any words.

I could, however, cry. And that's exactly what I did until the night became the dawn. Feeling bereft and utterly lost, I walked out of the hospital that morning in the midst of the early-morning fog, convinced that, once again, my judgment had abandoned me. I was devastated.

The following afternoon, I was back in therapy.

David and I eventually talked after the Big Reveal. We even worked together. He thought, he said, that he'd given me enough clues and that I would understand when I saw him.

Clearly, I hadn't.

Two months later he moved on to become a Fellow in his specialty at another university hospital in another state.

My heart ached for him for the longest time.

Some women, I am sure, could have and would have dealt better with the events of that night than I did. All I know is that you take who you are to every situation in life, and then you do the best you can. I did the best I could. Sadly—for both of us—I knew nothing about crossdressing, and I was horrified by how he chose to share his secret with me.

For the next five years, I buried myself in work, therapy, and raising my girls.

My judgment had failed me so many times when it came to men that I felt I owed it to myself and to my daughters to simplify our lives.

I needed to calm things down. Clarify our future.

And that's exactly what I did. I dated no one. I unlisted my number. I continued to work nights.

In solitude, there was safety.

CHAPTER 17

The Great Unraveling

The days drifted into weeks, the weeks into months, and the months finally into years. It seemed to all, myself included, that I had finally made peace with my diagnosis.

Along the way, I changed doctors. My new cardiologist was again a woman and also on staff at UCLA, but that's where the similarities with Petite Cardiologist ended.

New Cardiologist returned phone calls and emails. She also tried, with great success, to get me to see how gratitude for the life I was now living would go a long way toward helping me with the side effects of the cardiac drugs.

I still had days shrouded in depression, but they came with less frequency. The nausea, dizziness, and night terrors no longer plagued me. And even if I wasn't walking ten thousand steps a day, I was coming close. I'd even gotten back to the gym.

G and I had also started traveling again. The trips were exhausting, but enjoyable. Life had moved on and my diagnosis had become part of my life, rather than consuming all of it.

With all this good news to report, I was stunned when, two years after my diagnosis, I stood up at a formal dinner in Chicago and the room spun—with such intensity that I had to grab the back of a chair to steady myself.

No one had to tell me this time. I already knew my life was about to unravel all over again.

I called my new cardiologist upon my return to Los Angeles, and when she suggested I be retested, I put up little resistance. I was now an old pro. Whatever tests they wanted me to have were fine with me. Angiograms? No problem. MUGA scans? Easy. Echograms? Easier still.

It didn't take long for the data to show up: I had entered into a new phase of heart failure. The drugs, for all intents and purposes, seemed to have stopped working.

"Is there anything that can be done?" I asked when the phone call came.

"We'll increase the dosage on your Toprol," New Cardiologist said with calm assurance. "That's the most powerful heart drug you're on. Let's up the dosage and then give it a few more weeks."

"Why did this happen?" I asked, more afraid than curious.

"I don't know. Your tests showed us that once again, your cardiac vessels are fine. It also confirmed that your left ventricle continues to be the culprit. Sometimes as your heart ages, the drugs aren't as effective."

I was devastated.

That night, in the darkness before the dawn, I bolted upright in bed, grabbed G's arm, and forced myself to breathe. It felt like a thunderbolt had just ripped through my chest.

"What's wrong?" He sounded frightened.

Unaware that the massive sweat trails that already begun to leak from my scalp wouldn't end their journey until they reached the middle of my back, I started to cry.

It had been building, this thunderbolt, long before Chicago, but I had ignored all the signals.

It had started with a small but growing emptiness inside my heart. My children were grown and gone. G had retired, and it was clear that his consulting business, which had been successful for so many years, was winding down.

The life that I had known was disappearing a little more with each passing day, and now my cardiac drugs had begun to fail.

I'd become a wanderer in my own life, empty and uncertain.

I know now, though I did not know it then, it was this feeling of emptiness that had created the thunderbolt. That, and my unspoken fear: I believed my life was essentially over.

On the night the thunderbolt arrived, I was truly frightened. I didn't know how to answer G's question. All I could do was sob, "I don't know. I don't know. I don't know."

I cried most of that day. When I found myself still crying the afternoon of the day after that, I called and made an appointment with the internist I'd known for thirty-five years.

She agreed to see me that week.

⚬

"What do you think is wrong with me?" I asked after the examination was complete.

"We can run some tests, but really, I have no idea," she said. "I'll speak to your cardiologist, but I do think a therapist might help."

I cried all the way home because I knew something no one else could see: My life, like a large piece of woolen cloth, was being torn away from the bolt. It was being rent from top to bottom.

I made an appointment with the psychiatrist New Cardiologist recommended, but it did not go well. I think my expectations were a problem.

I was looking for someone to help me, but help meant one thing to me and something else altogether to the psychiatrist. I wanted to problem-solve through talking. He wanted to problem-solve through pharmaceuticals. Still, when he handed me the prescription, I shrugged and took it.

I was worn out.

Another problem, at least to me, was the fact that he was young—so young that halfway through the session, I remarked, "I'm sure you get this all the time, but how old are you?"

He smiled. "Is that really relevant?"

"I suppose not," I answered back with a faint smile.

But it was.

The young-doctor-whose-age-was-not-relevant never told me about the side effects of Zoloft. He believed the antidepressant would solve everything. One dose later, however, and everything was worse. Much worse.

He had mentioned in passing, "There might be some discomfort for the first few weeks."

Within minutes of taking my first pill, the discomfort announced itself. Adrenaline surged through my body and sweat began to pour out of my scalp, face, and hands. My heart rate increased; my breathing became shallow; and worst of all, I couldn't sit still. I paced the floor, sat down on the sofa, then got up and paced the floor again.

I sent out an SOS to the young doctor and was oddly reassured when he said, "This is pretty normal. I'll prescribe some Ativan. Take the dose I prescribe, and you should feel better pretty quickly."

In a way, he was right. I did feel better once I started on the Ativan—but not by much, and now I had an additional problem: I couldn't take the Zoloft without taking the Ativan.

I'd already learned with my cardiac medications that there's often a time adjustment factor before certain meds become effective. The literature for Zoloft said it would take approximately two months. I had no idea how I was going to make that work. I couldn't even take it for two days.

I was back to living life in The Temporary Zone. It felt like I'd been boomeranged into hell.

Chapter 18

The Tin Man

My life quickly turned into a battleground, and every morning it was game on. I never knew who was going to be the victor by the end of the day.

It wasn't long before Zoloft staked its claim. The side effects were brutal.

Every morning I awoke to a river of sweat oozing its way out of my scalp. I spent so much of my time sweating, I began a love affair with our shower. One a day was never enough. Two or three usually met the daily requirement.

G often responded to the sight of my wet head with a smile. "Oh, I was wondering where you'd gone. In the shower again?"

I was so jumpy and irritable I couldn't sit or lie still. I paced and counted the minutes until I could take another Ativan.

I called the young-psychiatrist-whose-age-was-not-relevant every day and cried the same lament: "When is this going to work?"

He had an abundance of faith in Zoloft and assured me that it would be only a matter of time until I felt the more positive effects.

70

Again, we were back to the one thing I wasn't even sure I had: time. I sweated. I paced. I cried. This went on almost nonstop for a month, and then one morning I got up with a momentary sense of clarity and made a decision: I was going to find myself new psychiatrist. And I did. And he was older. And he talked.

When my new-psychiatrist-who-was-older-and-talked said, "Studies from Johns Hopkins have shown that Zoloft simply doesn't work on a small percentage of the population," I wanted to leap out of my chair and hug him. I wasn't going crazy. I was, however, in that small percentage of the population for whom Zoloft didn't work.

Together, we decided that Zoloft was about to be history. But not just yet. First, I had to decrease my daily dosage every two or three days.

"Don't stop cold turkey," he said. "Otherwise you'll bring on another set of undesirable symptoms." And I still had to continue the Ativan.

One week into my new adventure of getting off the Zoloft, I stood up from the sofa and walked into the kitchen. With that one simple series of movements, my body declared, "We are no longer doing business as usual." My legs felt like they belonged to the Tin Man from the Wizard of Oz.

I pressed two fingers against my carotid artery to check my pulse. My heart rate was rapid and grossly irregular.

I wasn't frightened. I was terrified.

I didn't know what to do. I couldn't call G.

Well, actually, I *could* call him, but it wouldn't do me any good. He was out of town.

I could've called 911. Perhaps I even should have called 911. But I didn't—and do you know why? I was embarrassed. It's embarrassing to have something wrong with your body and not know what it is or if it's even worthy of medical attention.

Much later, I looked up the top ten reasons why women die from heart attacks. What I found said this: "Women often delay in getting treatment and fail to call 911 out of fear of embarrassment." Though I did not know it then, I was simply behaving like the women in the study.

My solution at the time was simple. I called my daughter who lived nearby. She arrived quickly and drove me to the emergency room closest to my home.

My Tin Man legs carried me into the emergency room. "There's something wrong with my heart," I told the triage nurse.

Within minutes of my arrival, the nurses had admitted me into the cardiac room, started an IV, and done an EKG.

The ER physician was soon at my bedside.

"You're in atrial fibrillation," he said. "We're going to give you a little time and see if your heart won't convert to normal sinus rhythm on its own. If it doesn't, we'll give you drugs to help things along."

"Is that why I feel so weird?"

"When your heart is in atrial fibrillation, nothing is beating as it should. Your blood isn't circulating the way it's supposed to. So you feel, as you say, weird."

"Well, why do you think this happened?"

"No one really knows, but sometimes stress will do it. Have you been under any stress lately?"

I didn't want to get into it. I only wanted my heart to settle down—and twelve hours later, after intravenous cardiac drugs and an overnight stay in the post-cardiac care unit, that's exactly what it did.

Before I left the hospital the next day, the cardiologist informed me he would be adding one more medication to what I now called my daily cardiac cocktail.

"Patients who go into atrial fibrillation may have a stroke as a complicating factor," he explained. "You need to be on Elequis. It prevents a blood clot from forming in your heart and breaking loose once you go back into normal rhythm."

"But I'm taking so many meds already," I protested weakly.

He smiled an indulgent smile and closed my chart. "The meds you're on are designed to remodel your heart. You're doing very well when you consider how serious your diagnosis is."

I liked the idea of remodeling. I just wish the remodel had less do with my heart and more to do with something I actually enjoyed doing. Updating a kitchen, or even or a bathroom, would have been fun. Any room, really, except my heart.

Chapter 19

Angel's Watching Over You

Now, I think, would be a good time to talk about faith. Specifically, mine. Because at this point, it was running on empty.

The God I had turned to every day and in every situation since I was five years old appeared to have taken His angels (along with a few of His archangels) and gone on a vacation. The break was, no doubt, well deserved. But it did leave me wondering who, if anybody, was left minding the store.

When I returned home from the hospital, I took inventory of where things stood with my life, my body, and me, and things were not looking good.

Here was my list:

G was a constant source of support. Good.

I was back to being depressed, nervous, and anxious. Not good.

Zoloft not only wasn't working, it was actually making things worse. Really not good.

My cardiac diagnosis was changing. Outlook? Definitely not good. And finally: Perceived support from God? Not so much and not so good.

I felt like I was being swallowed up by a large, cosmic black hole and the only good news was this: I was sure I'd hit rock bottom. Things, I thought, could not possibly get much worse.

A word of caution here: Don't ever tell yourself or anybody else, "I don't think things can get much worse."

Why? Because short of actually dying, there is always worse.

After my trip to the ER and my overnight stay in the hospital, my cardiologist called.

"I spoke with the cardiologist you saw in the hospital, and I'd like you to make an appointment at the office as soon as possible."

She had a light, calm assurance to her voice. Still, her phone call made me nervous. She never called me at home.

"Should I bring my husband with me?"

"I think that would be helpful."

My prayer life moved from directing God on how to problem-solve to one of hopeful anticipation. If He just showed up, I'd be happy.

The morning of the appointment, I sent Him a little Post-it note, just as a reminder:

Dear God. I really hate to bother you, but would you consider coming back from your vacation sooner rather than later? Everybody needs a little time off, and you probably need a vacation more than most, but I'm really getting worried. I just got this phone call from my cardiologist and I don't think the news is going to be very good.

I know I've tried giving you directions before on how to solve things in my life and that probably wasn't such a good idea. So right now, I'd be perfectly happy if you just showed up. P.S. If you're busy, feel free to send an Angel.

Did an angel show up at the cardiologist's office that day? Maybe. It was a hard visit. I just couldn't be sure.

The news was not good. We already knew my meds were failing, and now one of my heart valves had begun to fail as well.

"So," New Cardiologist said with her never-ending, quiet confidence, "I'm going to recommend surgery for you. They'll fix your mitral valve, and once they've done that I think you're going to feel much better. But first I'd like you to have some retesting here at UCLA. When it's something this big, I like to double-check everything. In the meantime, I'm going to set you up with an appointment with the head of our cardiac surgery department. Let's at least get on the schedule."

Worse had arrived.

Chapter 20

"Well, They Die."

I used to think surgery fixed everything. Now, I wasn't so sure. My surgeon friends loved the idea of "cracking open a chest," but over time that concept had become less and less appealing to me.

My appointment with the thoracic surgeon happened quickly. Like so many surgeons I had known in the past, he was direct and straightforward. Everything came down to my cardiac numbers.

"Based on your test results and how you've been feeling," he told me, "I think surgery would be appropriate. I'd like to at least get you on the schedule. We can always cancel. We'll review everything again once all your retesting is done."

A date was set. My anxiety grew. My days were still spent crying.

I wanted to feel better, both emotionally and physically—I just wasn't sure surgery was going to get me there. My cardiac numbers weren't good. I knew that. I felt that. My chest hurt. I was short of breath. My legs were swelling. And now there was the added factor that retesting might show different numbers. What if they were worse? What if they were better?

I called friends and begged them to pray. My anxiety was unrelenting. I met every week with my Bible study group and every week I cried, "Pray for me. Please just pray for me."

A week after I met with the surgeon, I had an angiogram and another cardiac echogram. This time when they did the echo, however, they started an intravenous line and used a contrast material.

"Why are you using contrast material?" I asked the technician.

With a glint in his eye he responded, "The better to see you with, my dear."

Years ago, Mr. Rogers used to say on his television program that if you were ever frightened or going through really scary times, you should "look for the helpers."

I was looking for God and His helpers everywhere.

If someone was nice to me at the hospital, I declared it a victory. If the nurses were able to start an IV without having to make two or three attempts to get into a vein, I was sure God had sent His angels to help them. I lived in a perpetual state of gratitude. I was too afraid not to. I thought if I thanked the Angels for the smaller stuff, it would leave God available for when the really big stuff came along.

(Obviously this is not a sound theological practice, but it was the best I could do at the time. And the really big stuff was coming closer every day.)

The call came five days before my scheduled surgery.

"Anita," my cardiologist said in a voice that can only be described as solemn and, consequently, scary, "your surgery has been put on hold. I need more time to go over all your test results, and once I've done that the entire surgical team will meet to discuss your results. Something just isn't adding up. I'll see you in the office at the end of the week and we can go over everything at that time."

I wish I could say that I received this news calmly. I did not.

I was born with a catastrophizing mind. It has plagued me all my life. As a young student nurse, every disease I studied only added a new layer of worry to my already existing distress. I quickly learned that I would probably never have an ordinary cold, because every time I got sick my mind immediately turned it into an upper respiratory infection with possible secondary pneumonia. I never got the flu or a simple stomachache; in my mind, I was always on the brink of having a small bowel obstruction or ruptured appendix.

So, with that in mind, after the cardiologist called, this is what I didn't hear: "You might not have to have surgery, and this is a good thing." What I did hear was, "They may have to do more invasive surgery than was previously thought. Or, they may pass on surgery altogether and in that case there's nothing more they can do for you. Either way, you're probably going to die."

The next few days were an exercise in agony. Nothing I did took my mind off the impending visit with the cardiologist.

I heard her footsteps in the hallway before she opened the exam room door, and although I've never been a shoe person, I was pretty sure New Cardiologist was. She seldom wore the same shoes twice, and I never saw her in shoes that could ever be described as practical. Stylin'? Yes. Practical. No. I loved that about her.

It reminded of a young nun I'd taken care of years earlier who'd become gravely ill. And as I was packing up her belongings to send her to the ICU, I discovered a pair of red lace trimmed panties. I loved that about her, too.

New Cardiologist came into the room and wasted no time addressing the reason why I was there.

"Well, we've gone over all your tests, and the cardiac team and I all concur that your surgery should be canceled. Your present-day cardiac numbers are actually better than what we've previously noted. They're not good, but they're better than they were a few weeks ago, and I think we need to proceed with the understanding that you can continue to improve these numbers with diet, exercise, and your medications."

I stared at New Cardiologist in confusion. "But I thought the surgery was going to help me. Now you tell me the whole thing is off and I'm right back to where I was when this whole episode started? I still don't feel well."

"Anita, all I can do is cite the most recent studies. Patients with your diagnoses—"

"You mean patients who have both heart failure and mitral valve prolapse."

"Yes. That is correct. We have found that patients with your present-day cardiac numbers don't do very well after surgery."

"What do you mean when you say, 'Don't do very well'?"

"Well. They die."

This news did not make me cry, but I suddenly found myself unable to talk. "Oh," was my only response.

At this point G, who was sitting in the corner of the exam room, stood in the gap, as he had done so many times before when I was unable to deal with the information that was coming my way.

"What would you like Anita to do next?" he asked.

"The same thing we have been doing, only with more consistency. She needs to be walking every day. The gym is good, but it can't take the place of daily conditioning. I know things didn't go well with the psychiatrist I recommended, but she needs to continue therapy and support somewhere. We need to keep our focus on the fact that for some reason her heart is improving, even if we don't exactly know why."

I left her office confused and uncertain. Had she made the right decision in canceling my surgery?

Had God shown up and I didn't know it?

Or had we just rolled the dice on my life and taken the biggest gamble of them all?

CHAPTER 21

Lookin' Good

During the absolute worst of my journey, I looked fine. No one looking at me would've ever known that something was wrong. In fact, it was quite the opposite. I began receiving so many compliments about my appearance that I started to respond to those who commented with, "You know, I'm pretty sure cardiac disease agrees with me."

My appearance didn't change my diagnoses, but it may explain why everyone—our adult children included—found it hard to believe that I actually had anything wrong with me, let alone something serious.

It was this constant comment—"Gee, but you look great"—that helped everyone, myself included, stay in some degree of denial about my condition.

Denial had morphed in my life from a large, meandering river to a gigantic wave that ebbed and flowed with ocean tide. And here is what I learned about denial through this experience. Where there is denial there is fear. Big. Time. Fear.

I was afraid in the days leading up to my scheduled heart surgery. Statistically, women don't do quite as well as men post–open-heart surgery. I thought that meant I was going to die.

Then, when my heart surgery was canceled, I thought I was going to die all over again.

I was depressed and scared by the fact that the only thing I felt was God's absence. Did He want the surgery canceled? Had He orchestrated the whole event? My mind kept telling me that He was probably here somewhere, but my heart continued to doubt.

If you believe in a Sovereign God (and I do), then you also believe that He must have known all along that this was going to be the outcome. I should have felt reassured, but I wasn't. My lack of faith only added one more layer to my already anxious heart.

It all began to feel like I was in the middle of a big-time throwdown with God. And that's when I remembered the Old Testament story of Jacob.

Jacob, though he was a mighty man of God, had done some pretty dubious things in his lifetime. He was scared.

One day he decided he wanted a blessing from God more than he'd ever wanted anything. So, he spent one entire night wrestling with an Angel of God in an attempt to get it.

When, in the early morning hours, the Angel finally realized that Jacob was never going to let go or stop fighting until he received his blessing, so he blessed him. But he also touched Jacob on the hip with such force that it left him bruised for life. From that night forward, Jacob walked with a permanent limp. He may have been blessed, but he was also wounded.

G and I left the cardiologist's office and walked the few short blocks back to the Westwood apartment we had leased for the summer.

It was hot; LA was in the middle of a heat wave. As we walked, I began to feel the smallest flicker of hope catch fire within my chest. The almost impossible thought of "what if" began its birth process in my mind.

What if God was going to leave me with a mark, much like He'd left Jacob? And what if, just like Jacob, I would forever after live a life that was bruised but blessed?

The problem was this: At that exact moment in time, the concept of my being blessed was so far beyond remote it hardly existed. Bruised? Yes. Blessed? Not so much.

CHAPTER 22

Here We Go Again

The phone calls from friends came almost immediately. "What? Your surgery was canceled? That's fabulous! Wait, is that fabulous?" Everyone shared in my confusion.

What was not confusing was that I needed to start back on my walking schedule—even if I became short of breath, even if my chest hurt, and even if I didn't want to do it. My cardiac numbers had improved, but not by much. I needed to build on that. If, that is, I accepted the new "wounded but blessed" premise for my life. A premise I wasn't even sure I was on board with yet.

My older-psychiatrist-who-talked looked solemn.

"Let me just clarify something I think you said. Maybe I'm reading something into it that not's there. I'm not sure. Are you trying to tell me you don't want to live?"

His question startled me. What had I said that prompted his question? I couldn't even remember.

The usual pleasantries of our fifty-minute therapy hour quickly evaporated.

For several seconds I sat and glanced around his office. Finally, I cleared my throat. "I'm not sure."

I waited to see if he was going to say anything in return. He didn't.

"I don't feel well," I continued. "I'm tired of not feeling well. I am bone tired of not feeling well. And I'm sick of having to give myself a pep talk every single day just to get out of bed. I can't think clearly. The cardiac meds keep me in a perpetual fog. You know that Billy Joel song, 'New York State of Mind'?"

The older-psychiatrist-who-usually-talked only nodded.

"Well, I live in a foggy state of mind. It's been that way ever since Chicago. If I don't take my meds at the same time every day, I feel lousy the next day. If I don't take them with a full glass of water, I feel lousy the next day. I have to do everything exactly as the pharmacist instructed me to do or there's nothing but trouble. I've talked with other people who take the same drugs and they aren't bothered at all."

"Have you talked to your cardiologist about this?"

"Yes, I have. She thinks I'm super sensitive to the medication. There's nothing more she can do."

"And you feel that if you can't take your medication without the side effects, life isn't worth living?"

I thought about what he asked for a moment. "That sort of makes me sound like an idiot. But I guess that's it. I'm sick and tired of being sick and tired. And here's the thing: I don't think it's ever going to get any better. This is it. I mean, I'm not dead yet, so I guess that's a good thing, but right now it's really hard being me. And I miss my children and grandchildren . . . a lot. They live so far away."

"How many grandchildren do you have?"

"Eight. Boys. We have a blended family."

"And where do these eight boys live?"

"Everyone lives in Southern California. It's a nine-hour drive from here."

He cocked his head slightly to the side. "I know you would love to change the subject, but could we stay on your medications for a second? Have you ever been tempted to stop taking them because of the side effects?"

"Yes."

He leaned back in his swivel chair and began to tap a solitary ballpoint pen against the center of his rather large wooden desk.

I had nothing more to say. He'd asked a question. I'd answered it.

Tap . . . tap . . . tap . . . went his pen.

Finally, he made a request: "Will you please call me before you decide to stop taking them?"

I wasn't sure what to say. I needed some time to think. Everything felt so muddled.

One thing, however, had started to come through with laser-like clarity. I was going to have to find some new coping mechanisms. The old ones were not working for me anymore.

"Okay," I said after much hesitation. "Fine."

"Fine?"

"No, really. It's fine. I agree to what you've asked."

"I have your word on that?"

"Yes." I glanced at the digital clock that sat perched on a stack of books on the floor in front of me. My fifty-minute hour was almost up. "Can I ask one more question before I go?"

He waited.

"Am I the only seventy-two-year-old woman in your practice with all these issues?"

For the first time that day, he smiled. "If I could show you my client list—which I can't—but if I could, you would see that many of my patients are in your same age group.

They don't necessarily have your cardiac problems, but they all have something. Many people are struggling to find peace and purpose in this decade of their life, Anita."

I sighed. "I guess that helps me a little to know that. Not much, but a little."

"Well, just remember I'm here to help, so don't be afraid to call me. I do think we need a little more time together. Tell my secretary to make an appointment for you for next week. If she tells you I don't have any time, ask her to call me."

Time. It always came down to time.

CHAPTER 23

I Sure Could Use a Massage

My search for new coping mechanisms started with a suggestion from my cardiologist at the end of my appointment: "You need to be in a support group."

It sounded more like a directive than a suggestion when she said it, but I ignored it.

At the time, I was overwhelmed by my geography.

I lived in a town of approximately three thousand people. It was rural, beautiful, and remote. It also had the largest natural lake inside the borders of California, which is exactly what my water-skiing husband had been looking for when he decided to retire. Water-skiing and all things boating had been a gift to our family life for years.

The fact that the lake was so remote made it ideal for water-skiing. Fewer boats meant fewer people. Fewer people meant longer ski runs. Great for water-skiing. Not so great for daily life.

It is a given that if you choose live in rural America, you must be prepared to drive. Everywhere. Twenty-five minutes to the grocery store. An hour and forty-five minutes to a Costco. Two hours to the dentist. Finding a support group wasn't going to be easy.

I searched online for days and made multiple phone calls. Finally, I met with success. The group I found was sponsored by the American Heart Association. It was also a two-hour drive and one small mountain range away.

"I'll be glad to take you," G said when I told him how far it was.

We went several times, but failure was built in from the start.

"It's just too far," I said one morning. "I've got to think of something else."

"What?" he asked with concern.

"I don't know."

My prayer group at church continued to act as an effective firewall between me and my growing sense of isolation.

My anxiety, however, left unchecked by the absence of Ativan, continued to run riot in my body. Loud noises scared me. I didn't want to drive. Even short trips to the grocery store filled me with tension and despair.

"My mojo is gone," I told G.

"Your what?"

"My mojo. You know. My mojo. I've lost confidence in myself."

"Well, I don't care what you think you've lost, you're still going to drive to the grocery store. Call me if you need my help."

And so I drove. And it was hard. And I did it anyway.

Now, did I feel abandoned by God? No. But I did have a strong sense that I'd been left by the side of the road waiting for the AAA roadside assistance truck to show up.

Jacob from the Old Testament might have been a first-rate success at living a bruised but blessed life, but I wasn't having much luck at all. Between managing my anxiety and living with questions that had no answers, life had become a tedious business. Would my cardiac numbers improve? Would I go into atrial fibrillation again? Was I really dying the whole time I was trying to live?

Eventually, I began to think that traditional Western medicine was going to take me just so far. I needed to try something new. Anything, really, that would redirect my anxious energy and clear the path for a new way of thinking.

And that's when I came up with what I thought was the perfect solution: massages.

Not just the regular kind of feel-good massages. No. I wanted to get every kind of massage my small town had to offer. And as it turned out, it had massage therapists in abundance.

I wanted to feel better—that was my big picture goal. But my small-picture goal was to find a way to reconnect with myself. I knew a calmer me existed somewhere. The me that had existed before I was diagnosed. The me that was capable and outgoing. I needed to create a new emotional home for that me to live in. A calmer home. A quieter home. A home where I could breathe.

And so, I began.

My first attempt was deep-tissue massage, and here is how I arrived at my starting point (or at least this is what I told G): "I need some really deep work to be done. So I think I'll start with the deep tissue first."

It wasn't exactly a well thought out, scientific treatment plan, but at least it was a beginning.

The massage therapists I saw were wonderful, but no matter how many times I tried the deep tissue experience, my whole body always ached for days afterwards.

I was encouraged to drink more fluids. I did. It helped. But not much. I moved on.

Next came the gentler approach of Swedish massage. It was pleasant enough when it was happening but did little to relieve my frustration and anxiety. Thai and Lomi Lomi were equally great, but I never felt a desire to return.

I decided it was time to branch out.

Acupuncture and chiropractic care came next. Yoga soon followed.

I still took all my meds with the required amount of water. On time. No deviation. I never had to make that call to my older-psychiatrist-who-talked. The one he'd requested I make in the event I'd decided to stop taking my meds. And I continued to walk—more on some days than others. And then, choosing the power of hope over experience, I went back to the gym.

During all this time, I never had the "aha" moment of insight where you suddenly understand why you were born and the whole reason God put you here on earth in the first place. I never woke up one morning and said to myself, "I've got it now. Wow am I getting better. Thank you, Jesus! I can take it from here." There was only this vague feeling that a candle had been lit in what was once a very dark room.

"Has the AAA Roadside Assistance truck finally arrived?" I wondered out loud to no one in particular.

I wanted to get better for G. I wanted to get better for our adult children and grandchildren. I decided to get better for myself.

Chapter 24

It's All Woo-Woo to Me

The flyer appeared one day outside on the bulletin board of the new yoga studio in town. A picture of a silver-haired woman was in the center and kindness seemed to radiate from her mega-watt smile. The flyer said she was a practitioner of Reiki massage. I'd had never heard of Reiki massage, but the flyer contained the magic word "massage," and that was good enough for me.

I took out a pen and wrote down the phone number.

Armed with that phone number and the picture of the woman on the flyer in my head, I went home, sat down at the computer, and looked up Reiki. What I read confused me. It's a massage, but it isn't. They lay their hands on you, but they don't. They talk about chakras, energy fields, and ancient Japanese healing—things I knew almost nothing about. But I did know one thing with absolute certainty: Once I explained it to G, he wasn't going to like it. He wasn't going like it at all.

My husband can be defined by the one word: traditionalist. His middle name happens to be Edward, but that it is simply a by-product of his birth. His middle name should actually be "Tradition." I think there is strong possibility he is descended from one of the Founding Fathers of our country. Even if he isn't, he thinks like he is.

If you were to meet him, you would probably say what most people say: "Stable. Smart. Really, super smart. Dependable. Salt of the earth. All-around good person." You would never look at him and think, "Free-spirited. Easygoing. Carefree. Great drinking buddy."

We've been married a long time. We met in church. All four of our adult children have, at one time or another, held positions of leadership in the church. One is a missionary.

From what I'd read that afternoon on various websites, Reiki did not fit in our family's vocabulary.

I decided the best approach would be to simply introduce G to the possibility of my giving Reiki a try. I chose that evening before dinner to do exactly that.

"What's it called? Reiki?" he asked with genuine interest. "What else do you know about it?"

"Well, actually, I don't know a lot about it, but I have read that people can get really great results from it," I said eagerly. "It's Japanese. Ancient. Really old Japanese. It's been around a really long time. Like, centuries."

"Is there anything else you can tell me about it other than the fact that it's old?"

"Well, I know they lay hands on you. It's sort of like a massage, only it's not."

G looked at me for several seconds across the dining room table. He looked tired.

"Do you have any idea how much money we have spent on your self-identified treatment plan so far?"

"Not exactly. Well, I mean, I know it's a lot."

"Thousands." He closed his eyes for a second and sighed. "I don't mean to say we can't spend the money for you to get well, but now you're off on some tangent, and who knows where it's going to lead or where it's going to end. And you don't even know this person who's going to be doing this . . . this . . . what did you say it was called again?"

"Reiki."

"Okay, Reiki." He studied my face. "I also think there's something more here that you're not saying."

I hesitated.

"Yes?"

"Well," I said. Aware that my lip had started to quiver. "I'm just not sure what it means when they say they work with your chakras. Do you know what that means?"

G reached across the table for my hand. "I have no idea what that means." Then he let go of my hand and shook his head in frustration and despair. "I know you're going to try this regardless of what I say, but I'm uncomfortable with all this talk of Reiki and chakras."

I knew he was going to say that. I lifted my chin. "Well, I'd just like to try it. I know that as Christians we're supposed to guard our hearts and minds, but I think there are lots of ways God can heal a person. I don't think it only comes through prayer or doctors and nurses. I mean, even in the New Testament it talks about Jesus healing people and he didn't even have to be the same room with them. So why couldn't He work through people here on earth?"

"You're talking about the Centurion?"

"Who?"

"In Matthew it talks about the Roman Centurion who goes to Jesus and asks Him to heal his servant boy. Jesus heals the boy without ever going to see him."

I pondered this for a minute. G knows the Bible so much better than I do. He seldom quotes it, but if you ask him a question, he can usually come up with the right answer. In any event, it's best to never argue with him on the finer points of Scripture.

"I think that's the one," I said with a shrug. "Anyway, I know we're talking about Jesus being the healer here, and not some lady whose picture I saw on a flyer, but I truly believe that I need to try everything I can. I'm doing everything Western medicine has to offer me. I need to continue to try something more. Besides, what's the worst thing that can happen?"

"The worst thing that can happen," G said with an edge of exasperation, "is that there won't be any end point and we'll be throwing away hundreds, maybe even thousands, of dollars on this stuff that's all woo-woo to me. Will you please promise me if you don't think it's helping you, you won't go back? I know it's been a hard road for you, but I think do think you're getting a little bit better. Don't you?'

"Well, probably a little bit. But," I quickly added, "I'd still like to try this person, whoever she is. Okay?"

G got up from the table. "I knew you were dead set on this before you even started talking. So it's okay with me, as long as you remember to walk away if you don't feel like you're getting any help. And keep the talk of chakras and all that other woo-woo stuff to a minimum, okay?"

Having made his decision, his mind quickly moved on. "Now, if we're all done here then I for one wouldn't mind eating. It smells really good in here."

It was settled. I was on to Reiki massage. Whatever that meant.

Chapter 25

Reiki Calling

Convinced that Reiki, even though I knew nothing about it, was the answer to all of the slings and arrows of outrageous fortune life had been throwing my way, I called the number on the flyer the next morning. My call went straight to voice mail. Frustrated and disappointed, I left a message at the sound of the tone.

I didn't want to wait for one more thing.

If anything held the promise of hope, I wanted it now. Right now.

Petite Cardiologist had told me I had to wait and see if my cardiac drugs would work. I was still waiting.

The young-psychiatrist-whose-age-was-irrelevant had told me I had to wait and see if my antidepressants would work. They hadn't.

New Cardiologist had told me I had to wait to see if walking would improve my heart. I was still walking. Still waiting.

When the Reiki therapist returned my call later that day, she told me she was booked until the end of the week. I took this as a good sign, oddly enough. I'd had no idea Reiki was so popular. I didn't ask her for more information. Nervous and hopeful, I didn't want her to say anything that could cause me to waver. I did, however, find out who she was. Her name was Bonnie.

Friday arrived accompanied by great anticipation. Prior to that day, everything I had tried on my healing journey hadn't worked very well or had only worked "wellish" enough. I was making progress, I knew that, but my "self-identified treatment plan," as G called it, really had cost us thousands. Still, I remained undaunted. Something was going to work for me, and I was determined to find it.

I also knew that the demands of my diagnoses meant I had to stick with Western medicine, even if the increased dosage meant the medication's side effects would continue to wreak periodic havoc on my body and psyche.

Eventually, I began to ponder a new question: *Do I really want to get well?*

All of the hours I'd spent in the office of the older-psychiatrist-who-talked had convinced me that I didn't want to die; but did I really want to get well? It's a good question to ask yourself if you ever find yourself dealing with an acute diagnosis that turns chronic.

Over the years in my nursing career, I'd often seen patients make return trips to the hospital. Some came to the ER so often that the staff had borrowed a name from the airline industry and started calling many of the returnees "Frequent Flyers."

I never asked any of these patients if they wanted to get well. It was never the time, nor was it my place. Jesus could do it—in fact, there were occasions when He did—but He's always had a better sense of time and place than I do.

Now, however, the time had come for me ask that question of myself. Did I really want to get well?

On most days my answer was yes, but the real question for me wasn't whether I wanted to get well, but rather, "What if you never get well? Will you be able to live in the Land of Wellish for the rest of your life?"

That was the question I struggled with daily. Sometimes I struggled with it by the hour. Sometimes by the minute. Sometimes by the second. When you added it up, it all came down to one thing: this was my life as I knew it now.

CHAPTER 26

It's Reiki Time

The first thing I noticed about Bonnie was that she looked, in person, like Bonnie on the flyer. Her silver hair turned out to actually be silver, and when she greeted me, the same energy that had stopped me on the street radiated through her smile and translucent blue eyes.

Her hands, slightly roughened from what she later told me was all her work with horses, said, "I'm here to help."

She worked from a small massage room that was connected to a yoga studio by a thin door. She apologized.

"From time to time we might end up sharing our time with a yoga class," she said. "I'll try to avoid it, but if it happens, just think of it as a happy accident.

"So, this is Reiki plus yoga?" I asked.

She smiled again. "Only until I get enough money together to get my own studio."

She directed me to some large purple and red silk pillows that served as chairs in the large, now empty, yoga studio. As soon as we sat down, she said, "Why don't we go over a few things before we get started? Tell me what you know about Reiki and why you called."

"Well, the first part is easy: I know nothing about Reiki. The second part is a little harder." I suddenly fell silent. In fact, the whole room fell silent. Even the birds outside, who always sing no matter the weather or season, seemed to have gone silent.

Bonnie smiled, an expectant look on her face. "Yes?"

"I called because I'm tired of living with my cardiac diagnosis and all the side effects of my meds," I said in a rush. "Everyone said the side effects would last only six months, but they keep adjusting the dosage, and every time they do I have a new side effect flare up. I'm also tired of not knowing if this is it."

"If what is it?" Bonnie's brow crinkled a bit.

"This!" I gestured to the air around me. "This life I've been given to live. Is this it? Is this how I'm going to feel for the rest of my life? I don't think it should be like this. I keep thinking if I just changed something about myself—and please don't ask what that would be, because I don't know—but there must be something I can do. Something deep down that can be changed. Some way that I think or feel about my situation that can be altered so I can cope better. When I saw your picture on the flyer, I got this feeling that whatever it is that you do . . . I thought it could help me."

Bonnie let out a deep sigh and suggested I do the same. As I complied, she said, "I am happy to do what I can, but I'm not a psychotherapist."

"I don't need you to be a psychotherapist. I have one of those. In fact, I've had several."

"That's good. I guess. Anyway, whether or not I'm able to help you depends upon the two of us. Reiki is a technique that works with energy. If you allow the technique to work, it can be a very effective healing tool."

I sat forward on my cushion. "And just how do I allow the technique to work?"

"You just have to relax and let me do the work. Two things I suspect you're not very good at." Bonnie chuckled, and (eventually) so did I.

"I'm not very good at either one of those things, as you have correctly guessed, but I'd like to try. Here's one other I think you need to know: my husband barely supports my coming here."

"Oh? And why is that?" She looked curious.

"Because I've already spent a lot of money on fairly traditional methods, and he considers this to be 'woo-woo stuff.'"

"Woo-woo stuff?"

"Yes. I'd never heard the word Reiki before I saw it on your flyer, and I had a difficult time explaining it to him. He's a pretty traditional guy. We're Christians. We met in church and we're still a churchgoing family."

"Well, I don't want to change your belief system, and I won't be discussing mine."

I looked at Bonnie, smiled, and said something from my childhood I hadn't said in a very long time: "Well, all-righty then." I was calming down.

"It would probably also be helpful to know," Bonnie went on, "that Reiki is not a fast-acting, take-two-aspirin-and-call-me-in-the-morning kind of therapy. It may take a while before you notice any benefits."

True to my nature, I let out a sigh of disappointment. "How long is a while?"

"That's hard to say. I think you've probably always been someone who would prefer to heal first and ask questions later. This may be a type of therapy that will work well for you."

"That makes no sense to me."

"It could be a life lesson for you. Healing isn't always an overnight sensation." She clapped her hands together and rose to a standing position with ease. "Why don't we get started?"

My eyes widened. "Wait! Don't you have a gown or something for me to put on?"

This made her laugh. "You're fine just as you are. All you need to do is take off your shoes and I'll give you a cozy blanket. Is classical music okay with you? I'll be playing music during our session."

Tears of gratitude sprang to my eyes. "I love classical music. I've loved it all my life. I grew up playing the oboe and piano. I was never very good at the piano, but I loved the oboe. I played it for years . . . just not very much lately. "

Bonnie nodded and smiled. "I think we are off to a very good start."

CHAPTER 27

Reiki Invades the Land of the Wellish

Bonnie was right. Reiki wasn't a quick fix. At each appointment she'd greet me with a smile, chat with me about my week, and then invite me to lie down onto the massage table. It was only after she'd tucked me under her cozy blanket that she turned on the music. I felt cared for and comforted, and soon began to wonder: *Has my heart finally begun to hear a new song?*

"You know," I told G one day after I'd returned home from an appointment, "there really isn't anything woo-woo about Reiki. She just uses her hands like any other massage therapist does except there's no real massage motions involved, and you don't take off your clothes. It's more of a laying on of hands than a massage of your muscles."

His answer was predictable: "Well, if that's all it is, why don't I learn a few of the moves and we can save ourselves a whole lot of money."

I didn't want to talk to him about how the Japanese felt you could channel energy and that it was possible to get better and perhaps even heal if someone trained in Reiki laid hands on you. Nor did I want to explain how they also believed that it was possible for illness to begin in your spirit. I knew G would think that channeling energy, unless it came directly from God in a Christian environment, was heretical. The church believed in the concept of laying on of hands, of course, but only if it was carried out by professing Christians.

I didn't quite know what to make of the whole thing myself. All I knew was that I trusted Bonnie the person. The process was just going to have to take care of itself.

When G asked, "Do you think you're getting better?" my answer was always the same: "A little bit."

Even if my healing was slow, something had started to change. I could feel it. Winter-like winds still blew through my soul, but for the first time in a long time my heart didn't feel so heavy, my head didn't feel so foggy, and the feeling of dread that up until recently had accompanied even the brightest of summer sunlit mornings had begun to diminish.

Reiki had invaded the Land of the Wellish. I was inching my way forward.

Bonnie wasn't very talkative. She was kind and gracious, but not very talkative. One day, when I asked her what brought her to our small town, she responded, "Oh, a friend invited me to try it out. I haven't been here long, but it's been a good move."

"I think you were sent here to help me get well," I told her.

Bonnie smiled. "I'm not so sure about that."

"Well, I'm sure," I persisted. "This town is too small and too remote. People just don't end up here by accident. I think God sent you here to help me get well."

"I'm glad you think so. It would be just fine with me if that were true."

Whether Bonnie had been sent there to help me heal or not, the side effects from my cardiac meds were finally becoming manageable. I still walked every day and took my medication on time. There were no deviations. At last, I was beginning to experience success in small victories.

⁂

One day, Bonnie asked me a question: "Have you ever tried Mindfulness?"

"I have not," I said. "I've read some articles on it, but I've never been tempted to try it. Should I?"

"Should you what?"

"Should I try Mindfulness?"

"Well, I'm certainly not an expert on the subject, but I do think it's something you might find useful." As always, Bonnie was gentle in her advice and suggestions.

I frowned slightly. "Is it like yoga? With lots of deep breathing and everything? Because I've tried yoga several times and I just can't get the hang of it. I don't know, maybe I just haven't tried the right kind."

"Why don't I just give you the name and number of a Mindfulness coach and the two of you can meet and have a consultation?" she asked.

I was skeptical. "Does live she far away? Because if she does, I know I won't stick with it.

Bonnie smiled. "No, she's local."

I didn't know what else to ask or say. I did, however, know one person who wasn't going to be happy about more therapy, no matter what it was called.

"You want to do more woo-woo therapy . . . more?" G sounded more confused than frustrated.

"Yes, but this won't be a forever thing. It's only going to be for now."

"Uh-huh . . . I'm not even sure I know what that means."

"It means I don't want you worry about how much more money we're going to spend because I won't be doing it forever, and besides, the really good news is the first session won't cost us anything."

"Well, here's the only good news in all of this for me: you haven't mentioned anything about the side effects from your meds in weeks."

"So you're okay with this?"

For several seconds, he looked at me without responding.

I repeated the question. "G. Are you okay with this?"

"Okay I think would be a stretch. Let's just see how this goes."

That sounded like an okay to me.

CHAPTER 28

Is All This Deep Breathing Really Necessary?

I am not a good deep breather. I am not a good meditator. I'm not even a good observer of the world around me, unless it is directly emergency room related, and then I am an excellent observer. Show up with a gunshot wound or a laceration and I will notice everything about you there is to notice . . . But that is not what Mindfulness is about. Mindfulness is about everything I'm not good at.

I met JoAnn on a sunny spring afternoon when all the dogwood trees near her mountain home were in bloom. When she greeted me at the door, her physical appearance surprised me. For no particular reason, I expected to see someone tall and commanding. But she was petite, with an abundance of wavy, silver-grey hair that fell well beyond her shoulders. She also had a radiant smile.

When she extended her hand and said, "Welcome, my name is JoAnn," I found myself wondering if both she and Bonnie had each received graduate degrees from the same university in Calm Assurance Smiling.

I also never thought that Bonnie's care and grace could ever be duplicated, but I was wrong. Here it was, once again, staring at me through the eyes of another stranger.

This was supposed to be an evaluation meeting for both of us, although I didn't know it at the time. I thought if I liked JoAnn, and Mindfulness was something I wanted to try, then all I had to do was schedule another meeting. It wasn't until I reached for my datebook at the end of the first session that I knew something was not quite right.

JoAnn gave me a curious look. "I see you took your date book out."

Her comment startled me. I waited for her to say something more.

"If you'd like to continue, that is something we both need to agree on. It's an invitation through discussion."

I gave her a blank look. "I'm not sure I understand what you just said."

"Let's take a minute and talk about what you liked about today. Did you like the relaxation?"

"I did, but I felt a little uncomfortable. I mean, is all this deep breathing really necessary?"

JoAnn smiled. "That's considered to be part of the Mindfulness experience. Do you think if I sent you a link to some of my work on the internet, you'd able to practice at home?"

"Practice what?"

"Some of things we went over today."

"You want me to practice deep breathing at home?" Uh-oh.

"I'm simply extending an invitation for you to try."

This required some thought on my part.

It was one thing to learn to Mindfulness in someone's office and quite another to practice it at home. I was skeptical and unsure.

But I really liked JoAnn, and as I'd discovered with Bonnie, if I trusted the person who was teaching me, I knew I would try to understand the process.

I decided to make the commitment to practice at home. A few minutes later, we mutually agreed that I would come back for another session the following week.

I am not a quiet person by nature. I never got A's for resting during naptime in kindergarten, and my mother frequently complained that she could hear me above all the other children at the playground. I never knew whether to believe her or not.

On the one hand it seemed too improbable to be true, but on the other hand, I thought, maybe she really could. After all, we only lived two blocks from the school.

Whether she could or could not hear me, her constant lament succeeded in leaving me with a lifelong concern. It's left me forever wondering, *Am I really too loud?*

To help solve this dilemma, I used to constantly test myself with others. I would engage people in conversation and then at some point quietly ask them, "Do you think I talk too loud?"

Usually they would answer with an odd look and simple, "No." But not always. And if they answered in the affirmative, it kept me in a continuous loop of low-level anxiety.

And yet choosing to stay silent was never an option. Therefore, I wanted to learn how to talk at a reasonable level, so I would be accepted. Which meant I talked, and talked, and talked.

When our church began offering silent retreats at a nearby monastery, I marveled at those who spoke of them with such enthusiasm.

Encouraged to attend by friends who'd found it life-changing, I always declined. "It's like fasting," I would say. "I can fast in the morning if I know I'll be eating by lunchtime. I could probably do a silent retreat for an hour or maybe two, but then I'd absolutely have to find someone to talk to. Do you think they have those kinds of silent retreats?"

My friends stopped asking me to go.

Before I agreed to practice Mindfulness at home, my thinking in JoAnn's office went something like this: If I wanted God to develop new coping mechanisms in me, even if I didn't know what those coping mechanisms might be, then I was going to have to put forth some effort. I couldn't keep doing the same old things that weren't working, or at the very least weren't working very well, over and over again. Reiki therapy was helping, but I continued to see my cardiac diagnoses as an erosion of my daily life.

Somehow, I needed to move myself to a new emotional address. I needed to see myself as part of the living instead part of the dying. I needed to see the world from a new perspective.

CHAPTER 29

Something Old. Something New. Something Borrowed.

Whenever I attempt something new, it is my firm belief that I should always try to look good even if I don't know what I'm doing.

If you had seen my first attempt at skiing, you would've thought I'd been hired to do a print layout for the Squaw Valley Ski Resort magazine.

None of my friends on the trip knew that all of my ski clothes had been borrowed—and sadly, it gave the wrong impression to the people who mattered most. The ski instructor took one look at me and placed me in an intermediate/advanced class, and even though I managed to make it through that ski trip without injury, the following winter I returned home with a fractured left leg and a long leg cast. For months, I remained on the disabled list.

Given my unfortunate history, you would think I would have abandoned my try-to-look-good-even-if-you-don't-know-what-you'redoing approach by this point. But this was *Mindfulness*, I reasoned. How dangerous could it be?

So, when I returned home from my first appointment with JoAnn, I immediately jumped onto the internet. I wanted to find out what the people who studied Mindfulness wore and perhaps find something for myself that would boost my confidence. And that's when I made a happy discovery: Mindfulness teachers, and even some students, wear very pretty clothes. *And* there are companies who make charming pillows for you to sit on while you practice deep breathing.

This was all going to be so easy! All it took for me to look as if I knew what I was doing was just of a couple of clicks on the computer.

There was also an added bonus, and it was this: everything fit perfectly in the area of the bedroom I had now designated as my Mindfulness corner.

With this commitment to my (as yet untried) new coping adventure, I was certain I would succeed. Unfortunately, there was one small problem: the internet said I had to wait seven to ten business days before the UPS truck delivered my new look.

That meant I wasn't going to be able to honor my commitment I'd made to JoAnn about starting my new Mindfulness exercises at home. What, I wondered, would she say to that?

Maybe, with any luck, it wouldn't even come up.

My next Mindfulness session began with what JoAnn called a centering exercise. That's where all the deep breathing started and that's where all the deep breathing would continue at the beginning of each new session.

I found myself conflicted.

While I enjoyed the process of learning something new, I was decidedly anxious about all the newness, too. I just didn't understand how deep breathing could change anything. I would have much preferred to use the time talking.

But Mindfulness wasn't about talking. Mindfulness was about being quiet—and so, as I listened to JoAnn's voice, I sent a quick Post-it note to God with a request. I asked Him if, assuming He wasn't too busy, He could drop by and show me a new way to quiet my mind . . . because I wasn't having much luck on my own.

I didn't want to turn God into my meditation buddy, because I was certain He had better things to do with His time. But I did really need Him to help me calm down and learn this new way of breathing. So I kept sending Him Post-it notes, one after the other. I kept them all really short, so He could just check them off as they arrived. *Please God, slow my breathing down.* "Check." *Please God, don't let me start crying.* "Check." *Please God, let me just focus on one thing at a time.* "No check. Sorry. That's going to take a little longer."

When the centering exercise was over, JoAnn asked me if I had any celebrations I wanted to share with her for the week that had just passed.

"Celebrations?"

"Yes. Big or small. Doesn't make any difference. Once you begin your Mindfulness practice, you may find you have a heightened awareness of your daily life experience. So, I'm going to invite you to think for a moment and then share any celebrations you might have had this week."

I thought this was rather an unusual request, since 1) I was the one who was dying from heart disease, and 2) I'd *wanted* to start practicing my meditation exercises, but I hadn't been able to yet because the UPS truck wasn't going to deliver everything I needed for another seven to ten business days (not that I'd told her that, and not that any of it was her fault).

That's when it began to seep into my brain that maybe I was a little more resistant to this whole new coping experience than I'd originally thought.

And so, we sat. And I smiled. And I cleared my throat and picked at the fringe of the purple lap blanket thrown across the arm of my chair. I didn't know what to say. I needed to avoid any reference to my failed commitment to practice mindfulness at home.

Finally, I thought of something.

"I signed up for a painting class on Wednesday. I'm not very good. Truly, I'm not, but I thought maybe I could try."

And then I surprised myself by taking a big deep breath.

Chapter 30

And So It Goes . . . Or Not

I eagerly awaited the arrival of the UPS truck.

Within minutes of receiving the delivery, I was seated on my new lavender meditation pillow in the meditation corner of my bedroom. My new black, boot-cut yoga pants and deep purple spandex T-shirt gave rise to the feeling of confidence I'd been longing for in my daily life. Now all I needed to do was to connect to the link JoAnn had sent me on the Internet, and my meditation experience could begin.

And so, I did just that.

I finished the centering exercise at the beginning of the tape and thought, *Yes! I can do this! I can meditate at home! I'm practicing meditation and it's working! I look like I know what I am doing and I'm doing it!*

But then my brain suddenly did a funny thing. It started acting like a ping-pong ball that had lost all sense of direction.

After the centering exercise ended, JoAnn's voice had invited me to close my eyes and keep them closed as we moved into the next sequence—and somehow in that one brief moment, I'd simply lost all ability to concentrate.

I started the meditation sequence over again. And again. And again. Finally, I gave up. I forgot all about deep breathing or closing my eyes. I decided to just sit there.

I thought that if I sat there long enough, maybe I would stop worrying about the irregular heartbeats that still plagued me on a daily basis. Or maybe I could stop obsessing about how long I thought I had left on my lifeline.

I stared at my new black, boot-cut yoga pants and looked at the clock on the bedside stand. Ten minutes had passed.

I didn't know what was supposed to happen, but whatever it was, my anxiety had trumped it all. I reached over and clicked off the computer. I glanced around the room. Everything felt the same.

My one solitary consolation was this: I might not know what I was doing, but I still thought I looked pretty good.

I made no further attempts to meditate that week. Everything was put on hold until my next appointment with JoAnn.

I continued to walk—even when I didn't feel like it. I still took my meds—even when I didn't want to. And I continued to see Bonnie for Reiki therapy—even though I really didn't understand how it worked.

Now if I could just focus when I practiced Mindfulness.

Chapter 31

Born Anxious

I have no celebrations this week. Not one. So, don't even ask me."
JoAnn smiled. "Why don't we wait until after our centering exercise before we move on to celebrations—"

"I couldn't even do five minutes on my own this week for meditation. I used the link you sent me and everything. My mind just kept popping off in all different directions. If the purpose of meditation is to calm a person down, how can you ever get there if you're not calm in the first place?"

JoAnn remained serene. "I think the fact that you're here says a lot about your commitment. So, if you're willing, I'd like to invite you to take another opportunity to try."

I stared at her and then stared at my hands in my lap. What if my attempts to meditate were all a gigantic waste of money? What if turned out that my anxiety was just a simple byproduct of my birth? Maybe I was born anxious and I was going to die anxious. Maybe I simply wasn't predisposed to being calm. What if peace and calm were gifts that God granted only to a chosen few, and I wasn't one of the chosen?

The thought alone made me sad, but my sense that it might be true made me grief-stricken. My chest felt so heavy.

And that's when a Bible verse floated into my head. I couldn't remember the chapter and verse, but I knew what it said. It said that God hadn't given us the spirit of fear but one of power, and of love, and of a *sound mind*.

Well, I thought, *a promise is a promise. Especially if it's from God. So I think I'll just have to work a little harder at the* sound mind *part*.

I looked up at JoAnn and nodded. "Okay. I guess we can try this one more time."

And that's how the process continued. Full of stops and starts. Frustration and tears.

I had to lower my expectations and raise my commitment to the practice of meditation on my own. I had to give myself permission to fail. Over and over again.

It took me months to learn how to sit quietly for ten minutes and not condemn my efforts to meditate for being too simple. Like David in the Psalms from the Old Testament, I wanted God to reassure me. Care for me. Comfort me in my hour of need and despair. So, I kept sending Him Post-it notes, especially when it came to my inability to concentrate during meditation, and over the next few months I eventually began to learn how calm down and carry on.

I no longer saw my cardiac diagnoses as an erosion of my daily life.

I knew they would always be there. I still had shortness of breath, swollen legs and ankles, and irregular heartbeats. On the bad days, it felt like I had my own syncopated drum section beating in my chest. On my good days, it felt like my heart wasn't sick at all.

In other words, I still had all the symptoms of heart disease, but the medication and its side effects had somewhat stabilized. Cozaar regulated my blood pressure with ease, but the dosage had to be constantly adjusted. Too much and my head would be swimming. Too little and my elevated blood pressure would give me headaches. My love/hate relationship with Toprol remained. But what insulin is to a diabetic, so Toprol is to a failing heart. Without it, I would descend into cardiac failure and eventual death. With it, I would always have to manage my depression and fight for mental clarity.

For the next twelve months, I attended Reiki and Mindfulness sessions regularly, and even though I still continued with Bible study every week, I chose to keep my healing journey to myself.

The fact that I believed in a God who could choose anyone He wanted to act as a healer didn't mean that others believed it as well. I loved the women in my Bible study group. Their prayers and support had carried me through some of my hardest times, even if they didn't know it. But not everyone agrees on how God heals. I knew that.

I had chosen a nontraditional path to a different type of healing years before I ever set foot in Bonnie's studio.

Four decades earlier, I had chosen to see a psychotherapist when my first marriage was in the process of coming apart.

At the time, psychotherapy and the church were virtual strangers. There were people in the church who felt—and still others who warned me—that accepting help from a psychotherapist was the same thing as letting Satan into your home. It was a hard thing to hear at the time, and even now it's painful to remember.

But I felt then—and still feel now, forty years later—that the psychotherapist was sent to me to be a healer. Just like Bonnie and JoAnn.

I stayed faithful to Reiki massage and Mindfulness practice coaching until I felt comfortable enough to stop going on a regular basis, and even then, I continued to practice Mindfulness at home. I was never able to sit on the purple pillow for very long, but I still thought I looked good while I was doing it, and if just showing up is half the battle, I was definitely winning mine.

When my older-psychiatrist-who-talked finally suggested I decrease my visits to his office to check-in status, I agreed.

On our final visit together, he walked me out to the lobby—something he'd never done before—then smiled and shook my hand. "You know where I am if you need me."

CHAPTER 32

Leaving the Lake

G and I decided to celebrate all of my good news by going on a cruise.

It wasn't the rough-and-tumble adventure travel we'd done in the past, but it was a chance to begin again. We chose Hawaii. A safe choice, we thought, particularly after my cardiologist reminded me, "You know, Anita, heart disease exists worldwide, and I'm sure if you run into trouble there will be cardiologists in Hawaii who can help."

When you live with a life-threatening-turned-chronic diagnosis, your world tends to get very small. You begin to feel as though you're the only one who has what you have. So the fact that there just might be others in Hawaii who also suffered from heart disease—perhaps even the same kind as me—was something I hadn't thought about until my cardiologist mentioned it. That they might even know how to treat it on the islands was bonus information.

Did I feel a little embarrassed that this information from the cardiologist was such a revelation? Yes, but I also felt comforted and reassured.

I boarded the ship with tentative confidence. G was ecstatic. We both were in agreement on one thing: we loved sailing on the open ocean.

Water ran in our veins.

Because water was so firmly implanted in both of us, it was odd that so many of our conversations onboard during this trip always came around to the one thing we had avoided for so long: We needed to sell the house and leave the lake. Life was forcing us into a transition we couldn't ignore any longer.

G still water-skied, but his long early-morning runs when the lake was nothing but glass were a thing of the past, and my skiing days had ended years earlier, after I'd first been diagnosed.

Our adult children and grandchildren continued to visit in the summer, but their visits were getting shorter, and there were some summers when they didn't come at all. They had begun the process of carving out lives of their own.

My ongoing cardiac diagnoses had now forced us to take a hard look at the truth of our lives. It was time to move on.

2

We returned home from the cruise encouraged by the fact that I had avoided any medical catastrophes, and ready, at last, to dive into the process of moving.

When we finally listed the house, we thought it would take a year to sell. It sold in five weeks. Life was moving us along faster than either of us had expected.

Once the date for the move had been determined and the movers had been hired, an odd thing started to happen with G. He began moving in slow motion.

He complained to me that he wasn't as fast as he used to be, and he wanted things to slow down. But slowing down was no longer an option for us. So I started to make him three-things-a-day lists. He didn't have to complete the tasks, but he did have to make an effort.

This worked . . . mostly.

Will-you-please-clean-out-the-garage-before-I-lose-my-mind turned out to be too big a task, so we took the garage in sections— one box, one corner, one shelf at a time.

It was tedious work. Moving always is. But eventually it all came together, and when our moving day arrived, G automatically shifted into the role he loves best: supervising.

His mother told me in the early years of our marriage that his ability to supervise and delegate was a gift he's had since childhood. She chuckled and added, "There were times when it worked and there were times when it didn't." On moving day, it worked well. Room by room, the house was emptied. Boxes were taped. Paintings were crated. Beds were taken apart.

We started in the pre-dawn hours of the July morning to avoid the heat, and by early afternoon I heard the doors on the moving van slam shut and breathed a sigh of relief. We were done.

Before the movers left, we signed papers that listed our household inventory. Not for the first time, I felt overwhelmed.

"G we have way too much stuff," I said as the moving van pull up the hill and out of the driveway and we turned back toward the house.

We planned to finish the day with one last tour.

Neither one of us spoke as we opened the front door. This was

a house that G had designed. It had won awards and been photo-
graphed by *Architectural Digest*. It had also been our home for fifteen
years.

Now, the silence was unsettling. Our footsteps on the hardwood
floors echoed and bounced off the plate glass windows that ran the
length of the house.

G kept staring outside as we walked. We had just reached the
halfway point on the stairs down to the kitchen when he suddenly
announced, "I need to sit down. I'm not feeling very well."

A surge of alarm jolted my body. "Does your chest hurt?" I
demanded.

"No."

"Do you feel sick to your stomach?"

"No"

"Does anything hurt?"

"No. I just want to sit here. I need to look at the lake for a while."

And so we sat, side by side, and talked. I could feel the depth of
his sadness.

"Are you going to be able to leave today?" I asked. "We could stay
at a motel in town tonight. We're not committed to any schedule; we
can do what we want." I was worried.

G cleared his throat. "No. I'll be okay. I don't really know what's
going on with me right now. I do think between the two of us, you've
always been the one who was more ready to do this."

"I just want to be closer to the grandkids," I said. "And my cardiac
status is so iffy . . ."

G nodded. We continued to sit and stare out at the lake.

It was stunning summer afternoon on the water. Ducks and their
constant companions, the black-headed grebes, bobbed like corks on
the small waves. Boats pulling skiers and wakeboarders swooshed

through the bay. Rock music blared from loudspeakers from some of the boats. Others simply took the time to drift across the lake with the sun high in the sky. Everyone, however, was looking for the same thing: the best water on the lake.

It was generally accepted by those who used the lake that you needed to be off the water by late afternoon to avoid the summer winds. Remain on the lake after the wind had blown it out and you could be in danger of swamping your boat. There wasn't anything about the lake that G didn't know or love. Even when the summer winds caught us; even when our boat engine stalled out and all the passengers had to jump in the water to swim our boat across the bay to home; G had loved it all.

"G?"

"Hmm . . . ?"

"You know, we're coming back next summer. We've left the boat loaded with all the ski equipment, and we still have to figure all of that out."

He continued to stare at the lake. "I know we're doing the right thing."

Then he stood and started walk down the steps again.

I thought he was heading for the deck outside the kitchen, but suddenly he stopped, turned toward me, and extended his hand. "Let's get this done. I want to make sure we don't leave anything behind."

CHAPTER 33

On the Road Again

B etween the two of us, G has always been the most comfortable with the open road. In the back of my mind loomed atrial fibrillation and heart failure. Roughly translated, its refrain was, "How far are we from the nearest hospital?"

While G felt we could handle anything that came our way, I was still afraid I'd wake up dead one morning. Clearly, it was much better to have him be the designated driver.

Once we sold the house, we'd updated our will and put all of our important papers into what G called The Death Box. I'd asked him if he could change the name and make it something not quite so grim. So he'd moved everything from the black Death Box to a white binder we now called The Life Book. Like our luggage, it went wherever we went.

The transition into this new phase of our life had been difficult, but once we locked up the house and climbed into our car, we both felt confident. We could handle what lay ahead. Whatever that was.

Our destination was a rental home in Palm Desert. It was not our plan to settle there. After all, where was the water? We just needed a place to call home base for what would surely be a brief time.

We are structured people. Between my German ancestry and G's need for control, "spontaneous" is not a word you would normally associate with us.

I had often thought that this needed to change.

G seemed so discouraged to be leaving our house that I decided now just might be a perfect time to risk something big.

What I wanted to suggest to G might have looked small to others, but to us it was huge. We were planners. We'd never been that-sounds-like-fun-let's-get-up-and-go folks.

The best approach to change all of this, I thought, was just to plunge right in.

"Hey, I've been thinking," I said as we made our first left turn onto the open road.

G glanced at me sideways. "Whenever you say that it usually means you either need money or you want at me to change my mind about something."

I increased the wattage on my smile. "Well, here's what I've been thinking. Why don't we take the long way down to Palm Desert? Let's get onto the 101 and head down to Monterey."

"Monterey?"

"Yes. Monterey."

"Couldn't you have said something about this a little earlier?"

"Well, yes, I could have. But I didn't. So now all we need to do is a simple little course correction. I have an excellent reason for wanting to do this. Do you want to hear it?"

"You'd better make this good."

"I think we need to practice hangin' out."

G looked confused. "Hangin' out?"

"We've never been very good at it. All the things that people do to hang out we don't do. We don't drink coffee, so Starbuck's is out. We don't drink alcohol, so wine tasting is out. And we don't play golf, so we can't even hang out on the golf course or the club house. We're both overachievers, and where has it gotten us in retirement? Nowhere. I've decided that retirement is one long adventure in hangin' out, and we need to get better at it. We need to find something to replace water-skiing."

"Nothing can replace water-skiing." G was not buying what I was selling.

"Well, I know that, but we need to work on finding something new and I think learning how to hang out will help us do that."

"And how is going down the 101 to Monterey instead of taking the 5 to Sacramento going to help us with this new endeavor of yours?"

"It's going to help because we'll go to Monterey and practice hangin' out there. We can go to the aquarium and then have lunch or dinner or whatever at one of the gazillion restaurants that are all over Monterey. We don't need to go the fastest way to Palm Desert. We can take the slow way and practice the whole way there. G, please. Just turn right when you hit Highway 29 intersection instead of left. That's all you need to do. One little tiny adjustment."

G looked exhausted. I could see that, but I honestly thought that if I could just get him to take a chance with a new direction on our road trip, then maybe a future without water-skiing might be filled with possibilities we hadn't even thought of yet.

He continued to drive toward the intersection of decision in silence.

I watched him and said nothing. I had said all I had to say. I was ready for it to go either way.

It wasn't long before I saw his face relax and the tiniest of smiles begin to creep into the corner of his mouth.

"You really want to do this?" he asked as he approached the intersection.

"Yes. I. Do."

With great flair, and even a little fanfare, G turned the car to the right. The vineyards of Napa, the Golden Gate Bridge, and Monterey were all ahead, waiting for us.

Both of us were stunned and slightly apprehensive when we began to see NO VACANCY signs popping up at almost every motel and hotel the closer we got to Monterey.

To settle our growing apprehension, we took a room at the first hotel on the bay that displayed a VACANCY sign. It also happened to be one of the most expensive.

When the desk clerk said the room would be $385.00, G simply took out his wallet and handed over his credit card.

"See?" he said with a glance in my direction. "Every time you tell me you've been thinking, it either costs me money or you want me to change my mind about something."

CHAPTER 34

What Was That?

When we awoke early the next morning, we knew we had a long drive ahead of us. Still, we were committed. Well, at least I was.

I asked G if we could remain at the breakfast table for little while longer after we had finished eating.

"We need to practice hangin' out," I said to encourage him. "I know it would be a whole lot easier if we drank coffee, because then we could just sit here and act like we're this totally cool retired couple, but take a look around you. This restaurant is beautiful. You can see the coastline for miles. And isn't it great to hear the sea lions?"

G glanced around. He was looking more and more uncomfortable with every second that passed.

"Okay, okay, okay," I finally said. "We can put off practicing until some other time. I know you want to get going to the aquarium."

"Does that mean I can ask for the check?" He shook his head. "I'm just not sure how this whole thing is supposed to work now."

"Of course, you can ask for the check! Besides I've been thinking—"

"Oh, no you don't." G handed the waiter his credit card.

I started to laugh. "No. This is an easy one. I think next time we go out for any kind of nice dinner or whatever, we should order tea."

"Tea?"

"Well, not *just* tea. I mean instead of coffee at the end of the meal, we could order tea."

"And then we could sit there and talk over tea?"

"Yes."

"Would that make you happy?"

"I don't know. We'd have to try it."

"Okay." G pushed back his chair to stand. "But you know what *I've* been thinking? I've been thinking this whole 'hanging out' idea of yours is turning out to be a whole lot of work . . . at least it is for one of us."

G loved the aquarium. Even the fact that every schoolchild in Northern California seemed to be there on field trip didn't bother him. The kelp forest, the ability to be up close and personal with the stingrays, and, yes, even the sea lions he had ignored at the hotel restaurant enchanted both of us. We left Monterey happy that we had decided to turn right instead of left at the intersection of decision.

Highway 1 still lay ahead of us with miles and miles of majestic grandeur. There was no hurry and little to divert our attention from the open road, the ocean, and the next phase of our life.

We threw the sun roof open and talked about what we both wanted in our next house and where we should begin looking. G liked the idea of mountains, streams, and clean air.

I needed to be close to medical help, wanted to be close to our grandkids, and, not for the first time, made a case for why it was important to me to have a Trader Joe's closer than two hours away.

G listened. I talked. G talked. I listened.

And when we both got tired of trying to understand each other's point of view, we turned on Vivaldi and watched the ocean waves crash into the rugged Northern California coastline we both loved.

The weather went from beautiful to spectacular as we drove farther south, and though G continued to suffer from an emotional hangover from the sale of the house, we both agreed we were heading in the right direction with our lives.

It was late in the day when the freeway signs told us we had just crossed over into the city of Santa Barbara. I was about to suggest we stop for dinner when all of sudden the oddest feeling announced itself from deep within the left side of my chest. It was as if someone had placed a Stop Work! order on my heart.

It was also accompanied by a distinct feeling that I was going to die. *Well,* I thought, *if I'm going to die, I think I should at least be sitting down.* Only I *was* sitting down. Nothing was making any sense.

"Pull over!" I yelled at G. "Please pull over! There's something wrong."

He looked startled. "I can't. I need to work my way across traffic first."

By the time we'd made it to the side of the road, the terror of the moment had passed, and it felt as though nothing out of the ordinary had ever happened.

"What just happened?" G asked, his face full of concern.

I shook my head "I don't know. I think my heart stopped beating for a few seconds."

"Stopped beating? What do you mean stopped beating?"

"I don't know. I don't know what I mean. Everything just went crazy for a second or two."

"How do you feel now?"

"A little strange, but okay." I checked my pulse. It felt regular and strong. "I don't think I need to go into the ER or anything."

"Well, I do." G crossed his arms.

"No, G. All they're going to do is run an EKG. They won't find anything wrong and my discharge instructions will be, 'Be sure to follow up with your cardiologist.' We'll have wasted four hours, maybe more, and I'll have been starving the whole time. We won't have learned anything new. And I'm sure my heart *didn't* stop beating, otherwise I wouldn't be sitting here talking to you."

I was irritable, and I didn't know what to do. Something had happened—but what was it? What could have come and gone so quickly?

G stared at me. "We're in Santa Barbara. I'm pretty certain there's a hospital close by. Maybe even two."

"No. No. No. I feel fine now. Really. Let's just sit here for a few minutes. Maybe my meds need to be adjusted or something. I think I'll just call the cardiologist in the morning."

"You'll call her? For sure?"

I nodded.

But I didn't call my cardiologist in the morning, and I didn't call her the morning after that, either. I was sick of hospitals.

I was tired of telling my story to doctors and in denial about what had just happened. I decided to put my trust in hope over experience. I was hoping it wouldn't happen again.

But, of course, it did.

CHAPTER 35

I Wish I'd Been in Nordstrom

No warning signs. That's one of the things that bothered me the most. Although, at the time, I wasn't sure what kind of a warning sign it would take to get and keep my attention. With migraines, I'd often get flashes of colored lights in my right eye before the disabling headache struck. So maybe there could be a warning sign similar to a migraine, or perhaps God could just give me the just smallest little shout-out. That could be another possibility.

For now, I had to content myself with the fact that these events would always catch me unaware.

When the second event struck, I thought it was a fainting spell.

Seeking refuge from the summer heat of Palm Desert, I'd decided to go shopping. Initially, the air-conditioned cool of the store comforted me. So what if I was lightheaded? "This will pass." I told myself. "It's only the heat."

But it didn't pass. It got worse.

In quick succession, I went from feeling like my heartbeat was slightly irregular to feeling like I'd been hit by a Taser gun—though in reality, I'd never received such a gift from any of the many LAPD officers I'd ever worked with over the years in the ER. Though they did occasionally ask in jest, "You want try it out?"

I wanted to sit down before I fell down. Unfortunately for me, there was not a chair to be found that day in Kohl's department store.

I gave myself two options: 1) find a bathroom and lie down on the floor until the room stopped spinning and my legs got stronger, or 2) try to make it to the car. I chose the latter. It was a good choice. The terror of the episode passed as soon as I approached the parking lot.

What I did next was as inexplicable to me then as it is to me now: I decided I would never go into another Kohl's again.

I was convinced that if I'd been in a Nordstrom or even Bloomingdales when this last event had happened, they would have had a chair. Probably several chairs. Maybe even an entire lounge with a sofa in it where I could have rested until I felt better. Somehow, I connected the severity of the event to the store's lack of chairs.

This made no sense, of course. But all I can tell you is this: In that moment, I decided I didn't want to die in a Kohl's department store. I didn't want Kohl's to be the tag line of my life story—something that would get repeated every time someone asked, "How did she die?"

Two days later, I tried to explain my situation to my elegant fashionista cardiologist. She laughed in response but quickly added, "Right now I think you have more serious concerns than if you ever shop at Kohl's again."

And then she sent me down the hallway to the Cardiac Electrophysiology Department, where I made yet another appointment for a consult.

Chapter 36

The Gray Area

New doctors meant new tests. New tests meant new information. New information meant . . . hope?

My two new specialists came through the door together. Well, not really together. The tall, blustery one came through the door first and immediately leaned against the wall, his arms folded.

The short, quiet one followed and quickly reached for the rolling stool across from me. I sat on the exam table. G sat in the corner. There were handshakes all around.

"So," Leaning Doctor said, "why don't you tell us what you think your heart has been up to lately?"

When I finished the quiet one said, "Hmmm."

"Both of you look confused," I said. "And I'm feeling more nervous now than when I walked in here."

They responded by asking me to describe the events again in greater detail. I did. This time I must have done a better job, because when I was done Leaning Doctor said without hesitation, "You need a loop recorder."

A loop recorder, he explained, is a small device about the size of a silver bullet.

"After it's implanted in your chest," he said, "it will record all your cardiac activity. That information will then be downloaded and transmitted to our office."

It all seemed so simple. Just one quick procedure and, as I understood it, we would have a new source of never-ending data. As G once said, "Who among us doesn't love data?"

I was stunned, however, when they told me I would wear the loop recorder for three years. "Do you think it's going to take that long to figure out what's going on with my heart?"

"Absolutely not," they answered almost in sync.

And they were right. Three weeks after the loop recorder had been implanted, we had an answer.

❧

Again, the doctors came in together. Again, we all took the exact same positions. No need for handshakes this time. We were all BFFs by this point.

"You're having short runs of NSVT," said Leaning Doctor. "It stands for non-sustained ventricular tachycardia."

I'm not sure if doctors learn how to cross their arms or lean against the wall in medical school, but I doubt it. It seems to me it's just a way of keeping a comfortable distance from the patient when you have uncomfortable news to deliver.

And this was definitely uncomfortable news. What he said stunned me. Whenever I saw ventricular tachycardia on the monitors of patients in the ICU during my nursing years, it was never good sign. String too many runs of V-tach together and you die.

A simple adjustment of my medication wasn't going to fix this.

"Doesn't that sort put me at risk for sudden death?" I asked. Aware now that beads of sweat had begun to pop out on my upper lip, I suddenly found myself hoping I'd put on deodorant that morning.

"Well, yes, it can," Leaning Doctor admitted. "But in your case, because your heart has already responded well to the medications, you're less likely to have that happen. Unfortunately, that also puts you into what we call the 'Gray Area.'"

I cleared my throat. "The Gray Area?"

"That's an area that doesn't allow us to treat these events. In other words, there's nothing we can do for your short bursts of NSVT unless they get worse. Essentially, your heart is too sick to ignore and too healthy to treat."

"By getting worse you mean . . . ?"

"If the events last up to thirty seconds. Right now, yours are lasting about five to six. Or if you pass out—that would be considered worse."

(Oh. No. Here come visions of Kohl's dancing in my head all over again.)

I said nothing in response. I didn't quite know how to sort it all out. Up to this stage in my cardiac journey, there had always been an answer. "You have a problem," I had been told, "and here's how we're going to fix it." I may not have liked the solution, but at least there was something they could do. Now I was being told there was nothing that could be done. Unless, of course, my heart got sicker. But a sicker heart also increased my chances for sudden death.

Leaning Doctor glanced at his watch. "Do you have any questions for me?"

"Yes, but it looks like you're in a hurry."

He shook his head.

"Well, I'll try to be quick. Why is this happening now? I mean, I've lived with this disease for a long time."

"We don't really know. I suspect age is a factor. I do think we should get a cardiac MRI. Your disease process has probably scarred an area of your heart, and if that's the case, the data from the MRI will help us if we ever choose to do an ablation."

"An ablation?"

"That's when we go in and try to pinpoint the source of the arrhythmia and eliminate it. It works very well in patients with atrial fibrillation, but not necessarily in patients with your diagnoses. Still, I think it would be helpful to have the information."

I was eager to do anything he suggested.

Even though both of the doctors spoke with extreme ease about my new diagnoses—"Let's just keep it movin', folks; nothin' to see here"—I felt that if I did nothing then every future irregular heartbeat held within it the possibility of sudden death. *My* sudden death.

The cardiac MRI confirmed what the doctors already suspected. My heart had been scarred by the cardiomyopathy disease process.

I had officially become a permanent resident of the Gray Area.

G reached out and put his arm around my shoulder as we walked out of the medical building. Between the tests and doctors' appointments it had been a long day, and it was still several blocks to the parking lot.

I was discouraged. I hadn't realized how much I had hoped there would be something more they could do. But G was surprisingly upbeat. As he saw it, our glass was half full.

"'Look at it this way," he said, giving me a squeeze, "your heart is so healthy there's nothing they need to do for it right now."

I, of course, was in a glass-half-empty mood. "Yes, but when these attacks or events or whatever you want to call them happen, they scare me to death. Not really to death, I guess. I think it would be more accurate to say they scare me *almost* to death."

When we stopped at the street corner for a red traffic light, G surprised me. He turned me around and put both of his hands on my shoulders. "We're going to get through this. We are. We've gotten through everything else, and we're going to get through this. But right now, I have a suggestion. I have been starving for the last hour and a half. I suggest we find a place for dinner before we go any farther. I think you're going to feel a lot less stressed about all of this if you have something to eat."

He made me laugh. "You mean *you're* going to feel a lot less stressed if you have something to eat."

The light turned green.

"What kind of restaurant might we be looking for?" I asked as we stepped off the curb.

CHAPTER 37

A Place for Us

Living in the Gray Area brought with it a sense of urgency G and I hadn't known before.

Finding a new home became a priority. We were still committed to making a life for ourselves in the mountains, and because we both wanted to stay in Southern California we started to look at the two most obvious choices: Arrowhead and Big Bear. Each were resorts with gorgeous homes and beautiful views. Each had lakes.

But I was totally unprepared for the predicament I found myself in every time we went looking for property. I couldn't breathe. Or rather, I could breathe, but it took a lot of work to get the job done.

When I presented this no-so minor fact to G, we both came up with the exact same question with no obvious answer: What do we do now?

I thought a good place to start would be with a call to my cardiologist.

"Is a move to the mountains even reasonable for me to consider?" I asked.

She paused for a moment. "I think the elevation of Big Bear is pretty high. If you really want to live in the mountains, why don't you look for something lower? I also think you should consider doing a test in our pulmonary function lab. It will tell us the highest elevation you can tolerate. That will give us a good place to start, and I think you'd find the information helpful."

I was surprised. "There's test that can give us that kind of information?"

She assured me that there was.

Hopeful, if quite not quite convinced, G and I agreed it was worth a try.

G, as he done so many times before, waited for me in the visitors' lobby while I completed the test.

He wore an expectant look on his face when I walked in. "Well?"

"Fifty-five hundred feet. That's it. That's as high as I can go. Big Bear is seven thousand. Arrowhead's a little less, so maybe that could still be in the game. I don't know. I think I should be discouraged, but I'm not. And I don't want you to be discouraged either. I feel like we have a shot at making this thing work. We just have to keep on looking. God has a place for us. I mean, if He could lead the children of Israel out of bondage in Egypt then I know He can find a place for us to live. All we need to do is change our focus and not complain if it isn't perfect. The children of Israel were always complaining. Even when God answered their prayers, if it wasn't exactly what they wanted, they complained. So, I think we should start looking at communities in the mountains at fifty-five hundred feet or lower."

I did my best to sell enthusiasm.

I wanted G to be happy. I also, though in that moment I chose not to say anything, was still hoping that wherever God put us, He would remember to throw in a Trader Joe's. But if He didn't? I promised Him that He'd never catch me complaining. Not once.

ॐ

We went back to square one and expanded our search.

Armed with this new data, we both studied real estate magazines and researched online with different eyes. What if we gave up on the glamour of the mountain resorts and started looking for something simpler?

And then G asked me a question one Sunday after church that surprised me: "Would you be willing to take look in the area where my parents had a cabin when I was in elementary school?"

"Forest Falls? You want to go back to Forest Falls?"

"Is that a yes or a no?"

I stared at him in amazement. "Sure, I'll go. I just never thought you had much interest in returning. Do you want to go with or without a real estate agent?"

"With."

"Sounds like you're serious."

"I am, but I need to you to be on board with this. We've been looking for months now, and we've done everything except look at Forest Falls."

I shrugged. "Well, let's start looking."

ॐ

Forest Falls sits at the base of the San Gorgonio Mountains. It's a drop-off point for anyone who wants to play in the snow in the winter or hike in the summer and doesn't want to make the long drive up to Big Bear.

At 11,500 feet, it is the tallest mountain in Southern California, but the base of the mountain has been made quite accessible to two small communities. It was there, at the base of San Gorgonio, that G's family had once owned a cabin.

His love for this cabin of his youth was one of the first things I had learned about him when we began dating. But the cabin had been sold years earlier, and he'd never talked about wanting to go back.

Still, I know that time changes things—so if G now felt the simplicity of a life in Forest Falls was worth considering, then I was game to try.

We'd spent so much of our energy looking for homes in the resort communities that by the time we got around to thinking that Forest Falls might be a real possibility for us, winter had already set in.

"This is nuts," I called out to G when he jumped out of the car to check the trunk. He wanted to make certain we'd brought along chains for the tires.

"Nah," he called back with more enthusiasm than I'd heard from him in weeks. "This is going to be great!" He climbed back into the driver's seat. "We've seen the cabin online. The realtor said she already has people looking at it. We've talked about this for days now. The elevation is perfect. Everything you could possibly need, medical or otherwise, and . . . *and* . . . that includes a Trader Joe's that's only twenty to thirty minutes away in Redlands. So if we like this place, I think we should make an offer."

Everything he said was true. Earlier in the week, we'd even given ourselves a self-guided tour of the area and liked what we saw. It was a casual community populated by kind and helpful people.

Still, I had reservations. "Okay, but here's the deal: If you like the cabin 'as is' and I see it as major remodel, are you willing to go along with me on that? I know you said you would, but are you *really* willing? I mean, the cabin is one hundred years old, and we don't always agree on what's charming, what's rustic, and what's just plain falling apart."

"The answer is yes," G said firmly. "But let's see it first. You're getting all worked up over something we haven't even seen yet."

"I'm not getting all worked up," I said, scowling a little. "I just want to be clear on this."

G threw me a sideways glance of skepticism and then announced with a smile, "Look, it's starting to snow. Good thing I checked to see if we had chains in the trunk."

When we arrived at the cabin we were greeted by the realtor, who was dressed for the weather in a dark green, mid-length down jacket and fabulous boots that said, "I do fashion and I do winter." Her smile was contagious and reassuring.

"Don't you just love this weather?" she said with a wave of her arms toward the sky. "I think it's just spectacular. The harder it snows, the more I love it. I'm so glad you were able to make it. Let's go inside, shall we? I think you're going like what you see, but if you don't you be sure to tell me."

I can't say we were awestruck when she opened the heavy wooden door into the one-hundred-year-old living room, but we did both feel a sense of excitement grab hold. We immediately looked at each other. Could this be it?

Later that night, we talked for hours about how much we liked the cabin, but "liked" was not "loved," so we decided to make a list.

Here were some of the pros:

We both loved the floor-to-ceiling grey stone fireplace in the living room.

G loved the forested property that surrounded the cabin and the fact that the backyard ran down to the creek.

I loved the large dining room windows that opened directly onto the north face of the mountain.

"It felt like I was looking out on a snow cathedral today," I told G. "A snow cathedral where I could breathe."

Here were some of the cons:

"We're going to need to add a bedroom and bath," G said.

"And do a major remodel on the rest of the house," I added.

To which G said nothing.

"G?"

"Yes?"

"I have a vision for this house. I saw it today, but it means that you have to honor your word about the remodel."

"And what kind of vision would that be?"

"I want it to look like a Thomas Kincaid painting."

"We don't even own a Thomas Kincaid painting."

"I know that! But what's that got to do with anything? I can still be inspired by the ones I've seen. Besides, you promised me."

G still said nothing.

"G! I'm not kidding you. I saw a vision today of what I thought this cabin could be, and it wasn't a hallucination, either. Now, I want this cabin and I think you do too, so I think you should say yes. Remember, you were the one who said we were going to put in an offer today if we liked the cabin."

"So what do you need me to say yes to?"

"Yes to everything. Buying the cabin. Doing the remodel. Everything."

"A remodel is going to be a lot of work."

"I know that. I just really believe that this is the place God has for us."

G smiled. "You really believe that?"

"I do."

"Then I say we put in an offer."

"You're good, then?"

"I'm good then."

We called the realtor that night and left a message. Three months later, the hundred year-old-cabin that sat in the middle of a forest and looked up at the north face of the highest mountain in Southern California became ours.

Chapter 38

Can You Hear Me Now?

Even though G and I both felt secure in the knowledge that God had brought us to this place—this cabin and this mountain—life in the remodeling zone was not without its challenges.

Still, I had promised God that I would not complain. No. Matter. What.

So, even after our first snow storm of the winter knocked out our power for over twenty-four hours and the only heat we had came from a fireplace fueled by a small supply wood that was now buried under two feet of snow, I did not complain. (I may have mentioned the word "Marriott" a couple of times, but I was very quiet about it . . . just in case God had dropped by to check in on me.) Nor did I complain when the second snow storm took down multiple limbs from a giant oak tree in our front yard and deposited them onto the hood of the red four-wheel drive Subaru we'd driven off the car lot two days earlier. And did I complain when the roof that was never going to need repair began to leak in the spring rains? No. I. Did. Not.

I didn't even complain when a six-foot-long black bear not only licked our bird feeder platter clean but also, once he was done, tore said bird feeder off the side of the house and threw it across the yard.

My only question to G at the time was, "Do you think we can find another place that's better suited for the bird feeder—or rather, what's left of it?"

Still, there were enough rough cardiac days along the way to make me wonder if time, for me, had truly become a luxury.

The NSVT events continued to plague me. In fact, they continue to do so to this day. As frightening as they still are, I try to remember to practice deep breathing and (as much as possible) to shop only in Nordstrom and other stores where I'm sure they'll have nice lounges.

I have said some variation of the same prayer, almost without ceasing, for years: "Jesus, please, please, heal me. And if You don't want to heal me then would you please make it possible for me to live my life without these stupid meds?" Jesus has chosen to do neither of these things, and I have to tell you, it's been a tad disappointing. But I know He has kept me alive against some pretty serious odds, which I'm sure at times has been exhausting for Him. So, there is that.

I have given up trying to figure out if I live in the land of living or the land of the dying. If I wake up in the morning and see G in bed beside me, I just assume I am not dead and the matter is settled.

I still send God Post-it notes. And I still look for the helpers, too. Every day. Sometimes those helpers are Mindfulness coaches. Sometimes they are doctors, nurses, and x-ray techs. Sometimes they turn out to be the check-out clerk at Trader Joe's.

Healing, I've decided, doesn't always have to be a complicated thing.

Our mountains wake up early in the pre-dawn hours of summer and don't go to sleep until long after dark. This goes on every single day, but not just for the creatures and plants surrounding us. There are children here. Hundreds and hundreds of children who come all summer long to the Christian camp at the end of the road. And what do these children do that brings such magic to these hills and this canyon? They sing.

They sing in the evening when the sun is setting, and they sing at night with campfires glowing. Their voices fill the canyon with church songs I remember from long ago and new songs I have yet to learn. And I love listening to them. It lifts my spirit and causes my heart to sing as well.

I have struggled my whole life to hear God's voice. I have searched for Him in so many hospitals, churches, and cathedrals over the years I've lost count.

But there is no doubt in my heart, as damaged as it is, that when evening comes to our mountain home and the music of the children's voices fills the canyon, my search is over. It's as though I know with absolute certainty that God has brought me here for one specific purpose. I am here to answer a simple question—one He has been asking me over and over again for years.

"Anita . . . can you hear Me now?"

These days, I can only nod my head and weep.

About the Author

Anita Swanson Speake was born and raised in Minnesota. She completed her nurse's training and began her nursing career in Minneapolis before moving to Los Angeles. She spent thirty one years working as a registered nurse in emergency rooms and intensive care units. As she finished her career in nursing she was looking for something a little lower in stress and found exactly what she was looking for at the UCLA Writer's Program and the Iowa Writer's Summer Workshop. Her first book, *Slow Hope: The Long Journey Home*, was awarded four-and-a-half stars by *Writer's Digest*. It also captured first place in *Taproot Literary Review*. Speake currently lives with her husband in Southern California, where she writes and tries to stay fit enough to keep up with her eight grandsons.

SELECTED TITLES FROM SHE WRITES PRESS

She Writes Press is an independent publishing company founded to serve women writers everywhere. Visit us at www.shewritespress.com.

Beautiful Affliction: A Memoir by Lene Fogelberg
$16.95, 978-1-63152-985-6
The true story of a young woman's struggle to raise a family while her body slowly deteriorates as the result of an undetected fatal heart disease.

But My Brain Had Other Ideas: A Memoir of Recovery from Brain Injury by Deb Brandon $16.95, 978-1631522468
When Deb Brandon discovered that cavernous angiomas—tangles of malformed blood vessels in her brain—were what was behind her the terrifying symptoms she'd been experiencing, she underwent one brain surgery. And then another. And then another. And that was just the beginning.

Hug Everyone You Know: A Year of Community, Courage, and Cancer by Antoinette Truglio Martin $16.95, 978-1-63152-262-8
Cancer is scary enough for the brave, but for a wimp like Antoinette Martin, it was downright terrifying. With the help of her community, however, Martin slowly found the courage within herself to face cancer—and to do so with perseverance and humor.

Body 2.0: Finding My Edge Through Loss and Mastectomy by Krista Hammerbacher Haapala
An authentic, inspiring guide to reframing adversity that provides a new perspective on preventative mastectomy, told through the lens of the author's personal experience.

Of This Much I'm Sure: A Memoir by Nadine Kenney Johnstone
$16.95, 978-1631522109
After an IVF procedure leads to near-fatal internal bleeding, Nadine Kenney Johnstone must ask herself if the journey to create life is worth risking her own—and eventually learns that in an unpredictable life, the only thing she can be sure of is the healing power of hope.

A Leg to Stand On: An Amputee's Walk into Motherhood by Colleen Haggerty $16.95, 978-1-63152-923-8
Haggerty's candid story of how she overcame the pain of losing a leg at seventeen—and of terminating two pregnancies as a young woman—and went on to become a mother, despite her fears.